MW00984751

A BREATH AWAY

A BREATH
AWAY

one woman's journey through widowhood

In the midst of winter,
I finally learned there was in me
an invincible summer.
-Albert Camus

CAROL LUCAS

Charleston, SC
www.PalmettoPublishing.com

A Breath Away
Copyright © 2021 by Carol Lucas

All rights reserved
No portion of this book may be reproduced, stored in a retrieval
system, or transmitted in any form by any means–electronic,
mechanical, photocopy, recording, or other–except for brief quotations
in printed reviews, without prior permission of the author.

First Edition

Hardcover ISBN: 978-1-63837-077-2
Paperback ISBN: 978-1-63837-078-9

Dedicated to my daughters,
Jennifer and Stephanie,
and to my late husband, Noel,
all of whom gave,
and continue to give,
unconditional support,
before, during, and after…
you are the wind beneath my wings.

ACKNOWLEDGMENTS

Most authors recognize that their work is not completed in a vacuum, and I am no different. I know that moving out of the pain of my loss and being able to write about it was directly proportionate to the strength of my support system, and I will be forever grateful to all of those who rallied round me.

My daughters, their husbands, and my granddaughters were a constant source of strength, and they provided light when darkness seemed about to crush me.

There were so many friends that were there to catch me when I stumbled: Marge and Marilyn, insisting I not return to my house alone when I returned to Beaufort but come to them, then and so many times after; Walt and Nancy who embraced me consistently and made it clear that seven was never one-too-many at a dinner party; Steve and Olga who were true guardian angels while we were in Baltimore (God does provide his emissaries); MD who gave me the courage to look in places I might otherwise have avoided; Christine Wicker, who made to me a proposition I could not resist, compelling me dig within myself and bring forth structure where only chaos existed; Martie, who made the past tense 'present' by giving to me the greatest gift a widow can receive; Frank and Shelley, who were so attuned to my needs and, by opening their home, helped launch me upon the journey of my life; Doug, Ian, and Jen who each, in his and her own way, gave us a sense of ease throughout our medical nightmare; and finally, the brave people who fought CLL and lost as well as those who valiantly continue the battle-my heart and my prayers are with you.

To the Low Country Women Writers: from the beginning you were with me. Your friendship and love as well as your suggestions propelled me to this place in time. My gratitude knows no bounds.

To Erin Miller, my project manager, and her cohorts at Palmetto Publishing: thanks for guiding me through this process and accommodating my "blips" on the screen.

And it goes without saying that I acknowledge my beloved husband who surely helped to make me what I am today, before his passing as well as after. I believe, without any doubt, that you continue your vigil, Noel.

Dear Reader,

Please know that this message is **not** a disclaimer. Every word that you are about to read has been chosen carefully, with an eye to unvarnished fact and to truth… above all, truth. Yes, the book is rife with emotion; one cannot write about great loss without exposing pain, and pain is very emotional. While I admit that impassioned events can sometimes blur the lines of reality, I believe I have been obsessive about rendering a work that isn't drowning in sadness. In fact, I hope you will appreciate the humor that appears within these pages every bit as much as the story itself, because I, too, experienced many times of laughter, when it seemed I would never smile again.

I know there are those of you who will approach the book with feelings and beliefs that range from skepticism to cynicism regarding after-death communication, and that is all right. I certainly would have billed myself as a skeptic prior to my husband's passing. That said, I ask you to temporarily try to keep those feelings at bay as you read, and know that I have made every effort to be exceptionally true to the actual events. For readers who accept, without question, the kind of events you are about to encounter, it is merely another adventure down a road with which you are already familiar.

At one point someone suggested that perhaps my book would sell more readily if I were to make it a fictional account. This would betray my husband in the worst possible way, and you will understand when you have read to the last page why I could never have considered this suggestion.

It has taken almost two decades to bring these pages together so that I might feel comfortable with every aspect of publicly divulging the most important story of my life. It is one of great joy as well as one of loss and anguish; certainly it is a personal validation of belief in life after death. Most important, however, it is a story of love so powerful that I have been able to seek love again with a high degree of anticipation and without guilt. For those of you who have lost and yearn to believe you can love again, I hope this book starts you down the path of enlightenment and gives you hope.

Finally, I ask that you please take time to read the quotations that appear at the beginning of every chapter. They are wonderful words, written by people so much more insightful than I, words that speak to your soul.

Best regards,
Carol

Death is nothing at all. I have only slipped away into the next room. I am I, and you are you. Whatever we were to each other, that we are still. Call me by my old familiar name; speak to me in the easy way you always used. Put no difference into your tone...wear no forced air of sorrow. Laugh as we always laughed at the little jokes we enjoyed together. Play, smile, think of me, pray for me. Let my name be the household word that it always was. Let it be spoken without effect, without the ghost of a shadow on it. Life means all that it ever meant. It is the same that it ever was; there is absolutely no unbroken continuity. Why should I be out of mind because I am out of sight? I am waiting for you for an interval, somewhere very near, just around the corner...all is well.

-Henry Scott Holland
Oxford Professor

TABLE OF CONTENTS

My love for you is a journey; starting at forever and ending at never.
-anonymous

PROLOGUE

if you must go, please stay in touch

If ever there is tomorrow when we are not together...
there is something you must always remember. You are
braver than you believe, stronger than you seem, and
smarter than you think. But the most important thing
is, even if we are apart, I'll always be with you.
-Winnie the Pooh
A. A. Milne

It happened entirely too often. As I repeated the words I had used on numerous occasions before, my voice would choke and my eyes fill. "I want to go before you do, Noel. I want to be the first to die. You have to promise you will let me go first, because I don't think I could go on without you." I was thirty-eight years old at the time, and I know now I was moving into a period of clinical depression that I would battle for well over a year before getting it under control. However, I viewed my persistent obsession as inexplicable apprehension that gnawed at me with increasing frequency.

My sweet, patient husband would sigh and gird himself for still one more exchange on a subject that tortured me and, as a result, brought torture of a different kind to him.

"You would be fine. Honestly, Carol, you would get along without me better than you think." This was the reassurance he always offered when I was hell-bent on broaching the topic of death...namely his. I'm sure his words were heavy with weariness had I bothered to pay attention. How many times had I relentlessly pushed him to engage in this conversation, always acting as though I had a new take on the subject?

"No, Noel, I wouldn't. I know in my heart you could handle the loss better if I were to die first."

"I'm not sure why you think that, but you know this is a dumb conversation at best. Neither of us knows what will happen, and even if we did, we have no control over it."

One day I must have pushed the envelope a little farther than usual. "At least promise me that if you go first, you will try to contact me from the other side if it is possible," I pleaded.

"Absolutely," he replied. "If you feel something grab your ass, you'll know it's me."

PART ONE

Now we see but through a glass darkly.
-Apostle Paul

ONE

enduring loss and embracing change

Look well into thyself; there is a source of strength
which will always spring up if thou wilt always look there.
-Marcus Aurelius

I read once that a man is more impacted by the loss of his spouse than a woman is. The theory suggests women are largely responsible for the majority of the daily life-supporting tasks around the house, and theirs is the central role of nurturer to the family. Thus their passing creates a greater loss for the surviving man. I am at once angered and amused by this assumption when I reflect upon the number of times I forget to take out the garbage- he rarely forgot- or I try to deal with the taxes- always his bailiwick. I don't even like to think about the time I had to negotiate with a car dealer to trade two used automobiles for a new one. I was completely out of my element and terrified that I would make a mess of the whole proposition. To diminish the emotions of anyone based upon gender is nonsensical at best and offensive at worst.

Let me make it very clear that I do not demean the emotions experienced by a man who loses the woman he has loved deeply. Furthermore, there is little value in hauling out the beleaguered thesis of Mars vs. Venus. Instead, I choose to believe any man who might read this book can find something to take away from it, some universal truth about love and loss and rediscovery. Undertaking the revitalization of one's self in the shadow of loss and sadness should never be construed as a gender-specific effort. The reality is grief is a difficult human condition that knows few parameters or constraints. With those disclaimers behind me, I will, however, use the term *widowhood* from this point on.

Life hurls painful challenges at every one of us, often with indifference that is both staggering and difficult to comprehend. Response to these onslaughts is generally one of 'meet or retreat'; rarely is there a middle ground. When my granddaughter, Alexandra, was three, she taught me a game she had learned in nursery school called "Goin' on a Bear Hunt." She would sit on the floor, her chubby little hands slapping her thighs, chanting, "Can't go over it, can't go under it, can't go around it, gotta' go through it." At some point after I lost Noel, this, subconsciously, became my mantra, and I began to recognize that I had to walk through my loss, endure the weight of my suffering, and perhaps even embrace my pain in order to make it to the other side. "Baptism by fire" is a well-worn idiom, and yet I believe there is nothing that more adequately describes the profound sorrow brought about by the loss of someone you love unconditionally. Very simply, the intensity of the experience sears you in a way previously unknown. After a time the magnitude of weight diminishes, the crushing pain becomes a static ache, and you emerge, ready to step cautiously onto the surreal stage of that theater-in-the-round called widowhood. It is how a woman acts out her part, a kind of reinventing of herself,that determines the extent to which she triumphs during the next phase of her life.

At first widowhood is much like being sentenced to wear an oversized coat

for the rest of your life. It hangs awkwardly in all the wrong places and is too long, causing you to trip over and over again. The only time you take it off is when you retire for the night, and even then it lies at the end of the bed, ready in a moment of unconscious thrashing to entangle and smother you. It can even yank you out of a troubled sleep, and when you awake, you are gasping for breath. However, as the days relentlessly march forward, you either grow into the garment or maybe it shrinks a bit, but one day you realize it does appear to fit better. The fabric is a bit worn, but it is noticeably more comfortable, and you gather it about your shoulders, accepting the familiar touch.

Managing widowhood is hardly an exact science; no two women share the same experience because no two marriages are the same. The relationship a woman enjoyed with her husband as well as the length of time she has been on her unique path will be reflected in her response as she grieves. One who is new to the nightmare and struggling to make some sense of it is the one who needs reassurance that her life will get better. It is she to whom I extend my hand and say emphatically, "You can do it! Cry, scream, rend your clothes if necessary; but when you finish with each catharsis and are so exhausted you can barely lift your head, you will come to accept this is a necessary part of your journey. Very simply, "You gotta' go through it." *And you will!*

I wish I could promise the content of these pages will remove the pain widowhood inflicts. What a wonderful gift that would be for all whose lives have been dismantled by the loss of someone so beloved. However, the book would necessarily have to include the potency of memory erasure, and ultimately that really isn't much of a gift, for it is our memories that sustain us even as they bring us to our knees. Rather what I hope to provide for every woman who feels defeated by her grief is a verbal embrace as well as a few insights **to** help turn her perceived defeat into a victory rather than a loss. If I can bring about the faintest smile or a flicker of recognition in these pages, then it will have been worth every moment at my computer.

I contend there is no pat formula for grieving. Certainly there are the accepted stages of grief as well as recommended ways to navigate the treacherous waters of each, and I don't deny those recommendations may work for some. I do not think, however, they are necessarily for everyone, nor do I accept that they get to the core of one's anguish or, to borrow from Joseph Conrad, the heart of [the] darkness. An acquaintance once told me, "Nothing in literature is right when describing widowhood," and her assessment is pretty much on target. It was this declaration, in fact, that pushed me to look closely at and explore the lonely landscape on which a widow suddenly finds herself wandering about, like the dazed science fiction character who awakens in a different time warp. Driven by my own experience, I felt the need to examine my surroundings as I made my way across this terrain, and it was here my spirituality was reawakened. As a result I was taken to places that before had merely aroused casual interest. Ultimately I became galvanized, and totally focused upon my investigation into what I believe was and continues to be my spiritual journey of discovery and peace.

In *My Losing Season,* Pat Conroy speaks of the value of loss saying, "Winning is wonderful in every aspect, but the darker music of loss resonates on deeper, richer planes," and he concludes, "I learned much, much more from loss." After reading those words, I rolled them around in my mind like so many colored marbles on a mirror, seeing the reflective beauty while at the same time feeling intimidated by the randomness of direction. If I could just accept the perplexing value-in-loss concept, I might have a better chance to understand and withstand my own loss. It took some time to fully assimilate the depth of Conroy's thoughts, but when I began to view my bereavement as something upon which I could build new connections to life, I became calmer and more content with myself. Admittedly this process didn't kick in right away, but every widow consumed by her loss needs to know that, with time, calm and contentment are attainable.

While I often thought privately my husband's passing was the worst thing that ever happened to me, I never stated this openly, because I have daughters and granddaughters whom I love beyond words, and tempting the fates is not a game I relish. The loss of Noel was, without question, an excruciating time in my life, testing me in ways I never dreamed possible. Yet this challenge produced in me some phoenix-like effects that included the realization of hope, both in retrospect and in the making. Revelations emerged from despair manifesting themselves in sometimes disconcerting but, more often than not, clear ways. These experiences invariably altered my viewpoint on a number of preconceptions I used to consider important. Thus over a period of time I grew, expanded my perceptions, and became a person I like better than I did my former self. Those 'deeper, richer planes' of which Conroy spoke provided a wealth of insight.

There are occasions when I reflect upon my metamorphosis, and while it wasn't an easy transformation, assistance was forthcoming, help I believe was rendered by my late husband. The events that occurred just prior to his passing, as well as those immediately after, and in the months that followed, make my story one of faith and optimism, a gift I gladly share. Mine is an account of personal discovery as much as it is one of loss. It is an affirmation grounded in the absolute belief there is life after this one, and I offer it to you, a glimpse of one widow's journey that is still very much in progress.

TWO

someone to watch over me

When you look you will find me.
I will be translucent flickering wings
between the earth and sky.
-anonymous

The solitary envelope lying on the white tile counter seemed innocuous enough, much of its bulk hanging over the edge as though it had been tossed there as an afterthought. However, it might as well have been a coiled snake poised to strike, and the sight of it instantly sucked the breath from my lungs, leaving me lightheaded. The envelope had not been on the kitchen island ten minutes before. I was as sure of that as I was of my standing there, and the shock stopped me cold. Was I becoming delusional or was something happening that went beyond the bounds of normal explanation?

A half hour earlier I had begun my search for this same envelope by engaging in an argument that, by all rights, was one-sided. "Where the hell are the canceled checks? Damn it, Noel, if I am supposed to do anything about our finances, I need those checks!" This outburst may have been nothing more than an excerpt from an unremarkable exchange between two people, but there was one notable difference, a huge discrepancy as a matter of fact. I was doing the venting, but the recipient of my frustration was my husband who had passed away a few weeks before in April of 2001. Granted, I had spent numerous moments talking to him, despite his absence, and I knew he wouldn't or couldn't respond. This was simply another time when I needed his presence, and it seemed that need wasn't about to be rewarded.

There was a catch in my voice, and I recognized what had simply been exasperation up until then was escalating into something greater. I was losing control, and it would be a matter of seconds before panic would overtake me- I had navigated that minefield many times before and recognized all the inherent symptoms of an attack. Having spent the better part of thirty minutes looking for the bank statement and canceled checks that had arrived in the mail days earlier, I thought I had searched every possible place where these documents might be. My eyes began to fill, and I shuddered as the death of my husband hit me with vengeance still one more time. Noel had always kept the checkbook balanced and dealt with most of the finances. His sense of organization reflected his scientific background, but now he was gone, and those jobs were falling to me. This was another cruel reminder of the impotence that had overtaken me in the months since I had lost the man who was the linchpin of my existence. I stood in the middle of the office with my fists clenched and lashed out, feeling the anguish wash over me.

Earlier that morning I was uncharacteristically focused, determined to complete something worthwhile that
I thought might bring some organization to my life, and at
the time it seemed balancing the checkbook could be a pro-
ductive undertaking. The day before I had managed to thoroughly clear the island in my kitchen, a catch-all place where
I pitched my mail as well as magazines and newspapers. The
large tile-covered surface held a daunting amount of paper,
so it took quite a while to complete the job; the end result
was worth the effort, however- a totally bare counter with
the exception of a cutting board and a spoon rest.

Walking past the island the next day, during the first
round of my scavenger hunt, I found myself wishing I
hadn't been quite so thorough, and it struck me then that
after yesterday's cleaning frenzy, I had managed to eliminate
a likely hiding place for the elusive checks.

Like the rest of my life, the realm of financial record keeping was chaotic. I had pushed the drudgery of bank statements
way into the background, deciding as long as the money was
there to get the bills paid on time, attention to detail would
come later. After all, I had spent the past couple of months focused upon the simple act of getting out of bed every day, and
if the morning were exceptional, I might even make it to downtown Beaufort, the pleasant South Carolina town my husband
and I had settled upon for our retirement two years earlier.

Thus it was I found myself in the upstairs office for the
second time, thinking I had probably thrown the checks in
question onto my desk. The truth was this area was hardly
pristine; nevertheless, I searched through the rubble again
and, predictably, was unable to find what I was looking for.
Thus I began striking out at Noel, wherever he was. Finally,

I went downstairs once more, willing to dismiss the entire project, and as I walked into the kitchen, I saw the envelope lying on the edge of the island. Admittedly my state of mind had been driven by unreliable highs and despondent lows since my husband's passing, but I was certain there was not a shred of paper on the kitchen island when I passed it earlier. Furthermore, only the envelope in question lay there. In the months immediately following Noel's untimely death, I had experienced other incidents I considered might be communication from him, but the inexplicable appearance of those checks was, beyond question, the most staggering.

I stopped and looked closely at the fat envelope, almost afraid to touch it, and I could see it was, indeed, the object of my search. Finally, I picked it up, expecting to feel a tingle, a surge of warmth, something to indicate those checks had turned up through unearthly intervention. While there was nothing unusual about the envelope, short of its magical arrival, I was so confounded by what had happened it took me several minutes to absorb the implication: Noel had felt my frustration and pain from wherever he was and had dealt with it in a way that was as straightforward as he had always been. I began to sob as the significance of this discovery struck me. I had been given a clear sign my husband was still very much around me, providing answers when there appeared to be none. Unwittingly, I had rid the island counter of every scrap of yesterday's clutter to pave the way for today's event. The anxiety attack I expected to take me down became, instead, an affirmation that carried me aloft to a place where I began to look at my so-called plight in life with totally different eyes.

THREE

shattered tranquility

*A woman's life can really be a succession of lives,
each revolving around some emotionally compelling
situation or challenge, and each marked off by some
intense experience.*
-Wallace Simpson, Duchess of Windsor

Anyone who has been diagnosed with a life-threatening illness or has had a loved one so diagnosed can tell you exactly where she was, what she was doing, and how she responded to the news. Much like the assassination of John F. Kennedy or the tragic events of September 11th, it is a freeze-frame moment. Noel, my husband of almost thirty-nine years, came home after a routine physical exam to tell me the results of a blood test taken earlier indicated he had what the doctor thought then was lymphoma. It was a gorgeous sunny Monday afternoon in November, but suddenly the sun went out; it was as though someone had simply flipped a switch. A sense of bleak gray immediately settled over my surroundings, leaving everything around me motionless.

Nine months before, having retired early, we built a new home on a golf course. Life was good, and all we had worked for most of our adult lives appeared to be settling into place. In a single moment that euphoria vanished. I stood in the kitchen with our toddler granddaughter hanging onto my leg, feeling as though I had been punched in the stomach. From that point on, life as we knew it ceased to exist. I called our daughter, Jennifer, and asked her to come for Alex, knowing I had to be alone to gain some perspective. Little did I know how convoluted this task would be over the coming months or where it would take me.

The details of Noel's illness are secondary to the telling of this story with the exception of those occasions at the end of his life when events took on new meaning. The disease he had was not lymphoma but, rather, Chronic Lymphocytic Leukemia or CLL, and it is incurable. I liken it to the Rodney Dangerfield of blood cancers, because for so long it has been thought to be a disease that strikes old men, one that probably won't kill them. Even today there are physicians who tell their patients if they have to have cancer, CLL is the "good cancer" and they will, in all likelihood, die as the result of something else before this disease takes them. However, during the early days marked by my frenetic research, I discovered CLL is indiscriminate of age or gender, and it is anything but benign.

From the time of his diagnosis in November of 1999 until December of 2000, when he was hospitalized with his first bout of pneumonia, Noel was asymptomatic. On one hand, this gave us some time to catch the collective breath that had been knocked from us when the notice of an incurable disease invaded our lives. On the other, I tend to believe as we moved through those months, we became somewhat complaisant. Visits to the local oncologist were a regular part of our lives; blood samples were taken, and we watched as the numbers rose and fell like the tides close to our home. Yet no treatment was recommended, because few symptoms were manifested. We played golf, hosted parties, and led lives seemingly normal and untouched by serious illness.

December of 2000 brought pneumonia, leukemia's bitter ally, along with what we believed was a good recovery, and we welcomed 2001 with gratitude. Noel lost a great deal of weight in January, and by February he had contracted pneumonia a second time. I knew things were going badly with his hospitalization and insisted he be flown to Johns Hopkins Cancer Center to be under the care of his hematologist, Dr. Ian Flinn. At the end of ten days we came back to Beaufort with the understanding we would return to Baltimore in three weeks for a CLL patient conference I was helping to organize, together with a friend whom I met online on the CLL website (she has the disease and, thankfully, is still living). My husband and I both acknowledged the time for treatment had finally arrived.

When we flew to Baltimore the end of March for the conference, Noel was becoming weaker and markedly drawn. Meanwhile I was silently grateful we were going to be at the facility in which we had so much faith, because I could see the dramatic downturn in my husband's health. Noel never made it to Saturday's conference because he developed respiratory problems, similar to those of flu. I wanted him to check into the hospital right away, but he felt if he stayed in his hotel room, he would be all right. Sunday was another bad day, but again he insisted on waiting for his scheduled appointment on Monday. My husband always downplayed the severity of his illness from the time he was diagnosed, because that was his way of handling stress. He referred to his situation as "just a bump in the road." Ironically, when he checked into the Johns Hopkins Cancer Center on Monday, too ill to walk by himself, one of the nurses used this same phrase, and he looked at me, smiled weakly, and said, "See, Hon, I told you." All of the fear I had tamped down for so many weeks suddenly erupted and washed over me like an errant wave that comes in much higher than anticipated. I desperately wanted to be calm for his sake and maintain an attitude that suggested that things were, indeed, going to be fine. Of course, it was my dear husband who once told me I should never go to Las Vegas because my thoughts were always clearly reflected on my face. At once my stomach rebelled and my brain signaled a range of thoughts that were more like screams. I'm sure I must have uttered a silent prayer, asking God to please let this be true. I held his hand, gave it a squeeze, and let the nurse take him back for examination. This was less than twenty-four hours before he was plunged into the comatose state from which he would not emerge.

FOUR

the longest night

*In the night of death hope sees a star, and
listening love can hear the rustle of a wing.*
- Robert Ingersoll

Retrospect tells me I tended to compartmentalize the last two weeks of my husband's life that ended with a night's vigil I now know was transformational. There was our arrival in Baltimore on Friday before the conference; the interminable weekend as I ran back and forth from the presentations to our room across the street, seeing Noel grow worse, becoming almost skeletal with each passing hour; his hospitalization on Monday; and ultimately the incident leading to his medically induced coma. This was followed by thirteen days of slow motion that felt as though I were struggling to get through a dense and unfamiliar rain-soaked forest, thick brambles tugging at me, impeding any progress. Those days became a slide show I played over and over in my mind for months after he passed away, and even today, years later, I can pull up many of the scenes on my mental screen in a moment's time: getting Noel out of bed on Monday by placing his hands on my shoulders, pulling him up with every bit of strength I had, and maneuvering him into the wheelchair for the short trip across the street to the hospital...watching his haunted eyes search mine as the nurses got him into the bed, those same eyes silently asking a hundred questions for which I had no answers... his young, brilliant hematologist speaking to me in a side room, when there was still hope, mentioning a treatment more harsh than originally considered... this same young physician hugging me as I cried because the three of us had come to know one another so well over the past year. Could I have done anything differently that might have edited the ending of that horror show? That was a question I would ask myself repeatedly.

The first night Noel spent in the hospital, the doctors tried to reduce his dangerously high white blood cell count through a procedure called leukefareses. In layman's terms, this involves removing blood from the patient and putting it through a centrifuge, thus removing white cells. The blood is then injected back into the patient. When I got to his room the next morning, he was partially raised in his bed and was very weak. He asked if I would give him some water, and as I lifted the glass to his lips, his head suddenly snapped back. The physicians who were in the room began working on him immediately, and I was quickly ushered into the hall and then to a nearby room. When the doctor came to that room later, the look on his face told me the situation was critical, and before he could say anything, I asked if my husband had died. Noel was still alive, but the incident required him to be heavily sedated. The brief time I had spent with him just moments ago would be the last I would ever hear his voice.

The next thirteen days were emotional chaos. A stream of people came and departed; I was aware of their presence but only vaguely. Our daughters, Jennifer and Stephanie, flew to Baltimore. Two close friends from Pittsburgh drove to see us, and Noel's sisters and brother-in-law as well as his mother were there and then gone. My mother and her husband arrived. Phone calls came from friends in Beaufort, and people I had encountered on the CLL website called the hospital and offered encouragement and prayers. Phrases like "making some limited progress" and "may have turned the corner" kept us holding on to the hope Noel would emerge from deep sedation. Occasionally he would open his eyes and look about furtively, but his eyes held such terror that the girls and I could hardly bear to watch his brief forays into semi-consciousness. We didn't let ourselves ask, "If he comes out of this, what will his condition be?"

Having my daughters with me during this time kept me away from the edge of hysteria. The three of us came together as one force, hoping we could will Noel out of the depths of the darkness holding him hostage. He was rarely without one of us in the room, and most of the time all of us surrounded his bed. My husband had always spoken of his harem with pride, especially when that bevy of females was extended by the births of two granddaughters. If our feminine willpower had been a cure, the man would have sat up, fully recovered, and walked out of the hospital on his own. Sadly, that simply was not meant to be. After five days, Jennifer went back to her family but not willingly. However,

I knew Noel would have been the first to insist her place was with her small children. Stephanie and I left the room so that she could have a private goodbye with her dad.

I have often reflected upon that two-week period of Noel's comatose existence and wondered if, perhaps, he had been taken to a place where decisions of untold magnitude are made. Did he navigate to the borders of this life and have to determine whether to leave or to return? When his eyes opened occasionally, always with fear and confusion, did he know what awaited him if he came back?

The morning of Saturday, April 7th actually brought some hope. I went across the street to the hospital as I had been doing every day, arriving around nine o'clock. As I sat next to Noel's bed and began talking to him, I took his hand and placed it between my two. At one point I felt pressure, and while I was startled, my immediate thought was his respirator had probably caused the movement. I felt the pressure again, and although I couldn't detect any visible change in his face, I thought he might be attempting to communicate with me. So I said to him, "Noel, if you are trying to let me know you are awake, press my hand again." It took a moment, but I did feel a faint movement, and I was jubilant because we had been given nothing close to this kind of response up till then. Then I said, "OK, big guy, this is a test. If you can do it, press my hand twice," and he did. There are no words to convey my elation and how grateful I was for this small bit of communication. I went to tell the nurses and anyone else who would listen, because for the first time I was encouraged by what had happened. Perhaps this is why the news from the doctor that evening seemed so incredibly cruel.

We had gone to dinner and returned to Noel's room around seven o'clock. Stephanie went in first and, unknown to me, spoke briefly with the nurse who told her the physician on duty wanted to speak with us. My daughter looked at the nurse and said, "He's dying, isn't he?" The nurse nodded affirmation, and Stephanie promptly went to the restroom and vomited up her dinner. When she came back to the room, the doctor was there. He began to speak of my husband's worsening condition, explaining that as sorry as he was to have to tell us, he felt all of Noel's systems were shutting down and he was dying. Stephanie was on the other side of the bed, and to this day I am not sure how she got to where I stood with the doctor. She could have bounded across the bed for all I can remember. My daughter is five feet, nine inches tall, and the physician in question isn't close to that height. Additionally, factor in that she had always been her dad's girl, and you can appreciate the scene that ensued. She told the doctor under no circumstances would we talk about this in her father's presence; she added she had read enough to know that hearing is the last of the senses to go, and we were not going to stand beside his bed and speak of his dying. It's odd how your mind shifts almost immediately into a protective mode when you have been given devastating news. My first reaction to this scene was one of embarrassment. My daughter was challenging a doctor from a world-renowned institution, Johns Hopkins, for heaven's sake, and I knew I had taught her better manners! My brain seemed to suggest if I could switch identities from that of a pending widow to one of an indignant parent, maybe this nightmare would right itself! Thankfully, the physician looked at her and said, "You're absolutely right, and I am sorry. Let's go out into the hall." That vignette is clear to me even now, and if it hadn't been for the horrific circumstances, perhaps I could have been somewhat amused at my daughter's audacity!

Can there possibly be any decision more guilt-laden than the one made when a loved one no longer has a chance for recovery and is simply being supported by medical technology? When the doctor confronted me with the unfathomable fact that I had to give permission for the removal of all the machines keeping Noel alive, I thought there was no way I could do this. How could I utter those few words resulting in the elimination of my husband from this world? Yet, Noel and I had spoken of this dilemma years ago, long before we envisioned such a scene in any terms other than "what if." At that time he had been adamant about my not keeping him hooked up to machines if his life was no longer sustainable.

Stephanie saw my hesitation and immediately said, "Mom, you know what he would want." I wanted to scream, "What about what *I* want? What about forty-four years reduced to this one decision?" Yet I knew she was right, and so I asked the doctor to give me fifteen minutes alone with Noel.

I have tried to replay that fifteen minutes in its entirety any number of times, but with the exception of clipped sound bites, nothing remains vivid. It is Charles Frazier who puts forth a noteworthy observation regarding the failure to recall that which is too painful. In the beautifully written novel *Cold Mountain*, Inman relates something told to him during his journey home: "It's a sign of God's mercy that he won't let us remember the reddest details of pain. He knows the parts we can't bear and won't let out minds render them again. In time, from disuse, they pale away. God lays the unbearable on you and then takes some back."

Perhaps the recorder of my mind erased the tape of those fifteen minutes because it is simply too painful to remember. I do know that I sat beside his bed, held his hand, and asked his forgiveness for what I was about to do. I told him I loved him more than my own life, and I wept inconsolably for the man whose existence, so intimately bound to mine, was about to end. Perhaps my tears were selfishly for myself. I pray that I kissed him, but my mind refuses to yield up that image.

The next few hours were more difficult than I could ever have imagined. Yet always, when I recall that time, I am grateful to have been afforded the opportunity to give to Noel the kind of loving send-off he deserved, and I now appreciate the concept of the Viking funeral when the cherished one is pushed out to sea. There was a CD player in his room, thanks to the insight of a good friend, and we played the sounds of thunder and rain for almost seven hours. Noel loved the thunderstorms of the South Carolina Lowcountry, saying they possessed a special resonance unlike anything he had heard before moving there. And so with sonorous rumblings as a backdrop, we talked to our husband and father, speaking of all the fun times we had enjoyed, never having to pause or search for incidents, because those times were legion. I talked of our golf games, our travels and our love, and Stephanie recalled many of the escapades that drove her dad crazy when she was growing up. An hour after we began our vigil his nurse came in to say for the first time in seventy-two hours Noel's heartbeat was regular. The irony wasn't lost on me as I thought of it later, and knowing what I now believe to be true, this was the beginning of his calm and quiet passage to the other side. As the night wore on, we repeatedly told him it was all right to leave us, that he had fought a good fight, and we knew he was tired.

At twenty minutes after two in the morning, I told Stephanie I didn't think I could bear to watch her dad flat line. She responded that I should consider leaving, but she needed to stay. Of course, I could not go either, despite the fact that I felt as though my heart were being slowly torn from my body. The pain was palpable for me. By then every mechanism keeping my husband alive had been removed, and his blood pressure was slowly diminishing.

Suddenly there was a harsh beeping sound from one of the disconnected machines that had been pushed unceremoniously into a corner. Because the noise was almost deafening, I told Stephanie I would get the nurse. As I started down the hall, Noel's nurse was hurrying toward me exclaiming, "I don't know why this is happening, Mrs. Lucas. Everything has been disconnected, and there is nothing that should be causing that sound." We both entered the room, and Stephanie was leaning over her Dad. She looked up at me and said, "He's gone, Mom." I think I recognized, even at that paralyzing moment, the eruption of the ear-piercing sound coming from the machine had not happened by accident. Noel knew how excruciating it would be for me to see his final moments of life disappear from a screen. Through some force not understood by those of us who remain here, the soul possesses energy as well as the ability to make an event like this happen. It was his last gift to me. Every bit as poignant was the feeling that took root with Stephanie. She told me later it was such a privilege to be the one who was with her dad when he slipped away, and I cannot help but think, just as he had done so many times during our lives, Noel orchestrated the perfect compromise for all concerned. This was simply the way he handled things, even his departure from us.

My daughter and I left the hospital and returned to our room across the street, walking through the cold, clear April darkness, accompanied by a security guard. I remember thinking it would feel so liberating to scream and scream until I no longer had a voice. Yet I knew had I tried, no sound would have come forth. Strangely enough when I got to my room and went to bed, I fell asleep immediately and slept soundly until the next morning.

FIVE

finding my way home

And I have promises to keep,
and miles to go before I sleep.
-Robert Frost

The term soul mate is overused and often misused, but I cannot think of a better descriptor for the man who was the center of my life from the moment we began dating. I was fifteen and Noel was almost two years older. The instant companionship we felt, even as young kids, went way beyond quick gropes in the car or dancing plastered against one another on a Saturday night. Noel provided a sense of calm that I had rarely experienced before, neither in my home nor among friends. While we relished the heavy breathing of normal teens who think only they know what it is to feel passion, there was a maturity that characterized our relationship, something that would serve us well and get us past the marital bumps and potholes we encountered later. Once during my senior year of high school, when I decided we both needed our space, I broke off the relationship temporarily. It was dad who told my mother in the colorful language he so frequently used, "Well, I hope she doesn't bring some sonofabitch home," which translated meant *any* other male. Both my parents loved Noel as much as I did.

Later when we married and moved to Pittsburgh, new friends would laugh and say, "Carol and Noel, the perfect Christmas couple." As newlyweds we were amused; as we matured such comments brought about the rolling of our eyes. The principal of the school where we both taught in the early seventies expressed his concern about having a married couple teaching together in the same building. Later, this man apologized and made it a point to say he felt we provided a solid example of what marriage should be like, a role model, he asserted, that was lacking for so many of our students. We knew what we had was special, and despite the occasional upheavals that most marriages encounter, we were able to get past them and remain best friends. I can remember a fellow teacher going on at great length about how he and his wife never argued. After he left the room, Noel said, "God, that must be boring!" and we both laughed. He and I simply worked well as a team, disagreements and all. Often, when he held me, I would tell him to keep in mind that no one fit into that space as well as I did. Now here I was, adrift on a sea of desolation I was totally unprepared to navigate by myself. How was I ever going to make a go of it alone? Fortunately, I did not have to.

It is amazing to me even today that the second child Noel and I produced together, loved beyond calculation, but often considered to be occupying the ozone much of the time, was the one to step in and take control as she did.

There was a time when Stephanie's version of long-range planning was deciding at six forty-five what she was going to do at seven o'clock. That she was able to accomplish what she did under such debilitating circumstances in the days following her father's passing ranks in my mind as a huge accomplishment. There were so many people to be notified. Additionally, we had to make arrangements for his body to be cremated, for this had always been his request. The next morning I listened as Stephanie called several crematoriums and in a detached voice made inquiries that would never have crossed my mind. While I worked in a trance, packing my husband's clothes well as ours, our daughter stepped up to the plate and organized when I could barely function.

Beaufort neighbors who had moved to Baltimore the previous year had been with us during the two weeks Noel was hospitalized, and they came to where we were staying, insisting we go to their home that Sunday night. Stephanie asked them to take me directly there, saying she would follow later in the afternoon. When she finally arrived at their house, she went to bed immediately, and when I went to the room where she was lying down, I could hear her muffled sobs. I thought then if pure pain could be distilled into an auditory experience, those cries I heard through the door would surely embody the sound. That night we slept in the same room, and around three o'clock in the morning, just twenty-four hours after Noel had left us, Baltimore experienced its first thunderstorm of the spring season. Stephanie and I both awoke to the rumbling, and she said in a quiet voice, "That's Dad letting us know he is okay." We had sent him off with gently rolling thunder, and now he was sending it back to us. Our daughter had traveled a very rough road during the previous day, making quantum leaps in her maturation. My guess is she felt the weight of sadness well beyond anything she had previously endured, and I'm certain her father was very proud of what she had accomplished. Because of what I have experienced since then, I can believe perhaps it *was* Noel's first communication to us after his passing. It certainly would not be his last.

When Stephanie and I arrived at the crematorium the following day, I had no idea Noel's body would have to be identified, but by then my mind was processing very little. I stiffened when the mortician spoke of this requirement, because I didn't know how I could view the stilled body of the man who had always been so full of life. Stephanie saw my panic and insisted she would prefer to make the identification. Later, when we were navigating our way around Washington, DC, she said the thought running through her mind as she went into the room where he lay was, "What if it is the wrong body and I start to laugh?" Of course this wasn't the case, and she told me she kissed her fingers, touched her dad's forehead and said, "I'll see you later, Handsome." I become very sad even now when I think about this, partly because the scene, as I envision it, is so torturous, but all the more so because I was unable to perform the task that she so bravely undertook.

I still refer to our trip back to Beaufort as a "Thelma and Louise journey." We drove as far as North Carolina and stayed for the night. When I returned from the hotel to the car after booking a room, Stephanie looked at me, nodded toward the container holding Noel's ashes, and said, "I guess we had better take him in with us, because with our luck the car will be stolen, and that would really piss him off!" I started to laugh and replied, "Unfortunately I made a reservation for just two." She responded, "Let's give the night clerk a thrill and introduce him to Dad." By the time we got to the room, we were both hysterical, a more-than-adequate description, as we fell onto the beds consumed with laughter. This was a much-needed release for both of us. When we called my older daughter to tell her where we were staying, she told her husband when she hung up the phone, "They have either gone completely around the bend or they are *very* drunk!" The answer to both assumptions was "yes," because we spent the rest of the evening consuming copious amounts of wine with the hope of dulling the pain produced by the loss we were both feeling.

The next day we drove on to Greenville, South Carolina and spent time with Jennifer and her family. They, too, were grieving the loss of a very special person in their lives. It was Alexandra, my older granddaughter, who ran to me as I got out of the car and asked whether or not I knew that Pop Pop had gone to heaven. As I held her tightly to me, I answered that I did know. "But Nana, did you know he became a beautiful angel?" she asked. I thought my heart would break, but that declaration became the hook upon which I would hang my thoughts in the months to come.

And so it was that a few days later I returned to our home in Beaufort on my fifty-ninth birthday, almost a month after having departed to take my husband for what I thought would be the start of treatment for his leukemia. I was widowed, bewildered, and not sure how I was supposed to go on with my life.

SIX

the last rave review

The truth is more important than the facts.
-Frank Lloyd Wright

When I arrived home and tried to settle into the new skin that was raw to my touch, there were so many issues confronting me that my ability to prioritize was skewed everywhere I turned. Noel and I had left three weeks earlier as a couple, and I believed we would be gone for what I hoped would be a brief period of time, although realistically I knew my husband faced immediate treatment, perhaps very strong radiation and chemotherapy. At the time, the challenge of getting him into the right protocol was all that concerned me. It never crossed my mind when we boarded the plane bound for Baltimore that I might return alone with my husband's ashes beside me.

There were friends who kept in daily touch throughout the horror of those days as I watched Noel gradually leave this life, and it was those same friends who cleaned my house and restocked my refrigerator, leaving on the table a bouquet of flowers for my birthday, the day I returned. These gestures brought about the first of many tears as I tried to reconcile my grief with the protective care that was so generously given.

After a few days of trying to rid my brain of the disorientation that had padlocked my senses, I knew I had to write Noel's obituary for both the local paper and the *Pittsburgh Post-Gazette*. We had lived in Pittsburgh for thirty-five years and had so many friends there; it would have been unthinkable to ignore that part of our lives. And so I sat down and put pen to paper to create a final tribute to the man who had been in my life for over four decades, my husband and my best friend.

When a woman addresses the task of writing an obituary for the man she has loved passionately, in many ways she writes her own death notice as well. Just as the words she selects tell of the person who is gone, so do those same words most assuredly hold unspoken volumes about the woman, herself. The process of composing has always delighted me, and I relish this challenge unlike any other creative endeavor. It causes some unspecified button within to be pushed, and the juices begin to flow, bringing together my mind and my heart in what I commit to paper. Yet I was totally confounded by the task of writing Noel's obituary, because I could not wrap my mind around words commensurate with how I felt. Some might say I was partly in denial, but I don't believe this was the case. I knew all too well what had happened, to me and to our daughters. Nothing in my brain let me forget the out-of-control train that had derailed and slammed into all of us so unexpectedly.

Shortly after my husband was diagnosed with leukemia seventeen months earlier, I found myself reading the local obituaries almost every day. I had never given much thought to death notices before then, nor had I read them with any regularity. Yet for some reason after Noel became ill, I turned to this section of the paper right away and immediately looked for the age of the person who had passed away. In a mindset that was unquestionably strange, I began playing the odds. If in a week's time I noted that quite a few of the people who had died were younger than sixty-five, I told myself God was close to filling his quota of people in Noel's age bracket. This mind torture began long before my husband showed any symptoms of his illness, and I could never bring myself to tell him of my daily visits to the "casino de muerte." How could I? What possible explanation could I offer for this irrational and obsessive response to the demise of others? When I look back on my behavior, I am astounded by the presumption, even if it was just between God and me and the paper on which it was printed.

It seems to me that the obituary is an oddly sterile method of announcing an event rife with intense emotion. Mr. So-and-So died on a particular day. He was born in the year of, the son of, survived by, and so it reads. The piece concludes with the name of a funeral home that is 'in charge.' In charge? How does anyone take charge of something as inexplicable and seemingly final as death? How can one wrest control of a person's demise and impose structure upon it?"

We in the Western world tend to ignore death until we no longer have a choice, and even then, the scene in any funeral home where the body is viewed by friends and family is often a study in quiet, subdued motion and emotion. Folks come in tentatively and make their way to the family, obviously at a loss for words. They may or may not go to the casket, and those who do choose to view the body, some with averted eyes, seem compelled to say how good the deceased looks, all the while knowing these words are insufficient, if not downright bizarre. If, however, you watch people from other cultures mourn their dead, you know there is a stark contrast to the Western way. They wail and beat their chests, men and women alike, flinging themselves about as though their hearts have been hacked from their bodies, and much like beheaded chickens, they appear to be in the last throes of dying themselves. Their mourning is overt and participatory. Western civilization rarely shows anything close to this kind of emotion, choosing instead the Puritanical stiff-upper-lip approach. So is it any wonder the final few murmurings regarding a person's life, printed in black and white and relegated to an obscure page of the newspaper, are mundane and completely disregard the Technicolor panorama of moving events that may have defined that person's existence?

I knew when I put myself to the painful task of writing Noel's obituary I would never be satisfied with the end result. How could I possibly convey within the limits of a small rectangle of newsprint the depth of goodness that resided within this gentle human being? There was so much more to the man than the banal facts; there was a love story with a very sad, very premature conclusion. Yet I had to accomplish this task to the best of my ability, and so I began.

Noel John Lucas passed away on April 8, 2001 from complications of Chronic Lymphocytic Leukemia. He was a 1962 graduate of Clarion State College *and I attended college there at the same time... our time spent together in this idyllic setting was as golden as the leaves that blanketed campus every fall... we both sang in the college choir and delighted in the various trips the choral group made to give performances... the last year he was there we planned our wedding and I hated it when he graduated first and left me on my own because college life wasn't the same without him.*

He earned a Master's Degree at the University of Notre Dame *and they permitted women to attend the university during summer school so I was able to take classes there as well... we packed our car to capacity every summer and traveled west to live in South Bend for six weeks... neither of us was Catholic yet we learned just how human the nuns and priests could be especially when playing softball or drinking beer... the last summer we were there I didn't take classes because I was pregnant with our first child and flew out of and back to Pittsburgh while he drove alone both ways... having a Notre Dame license plate on our car was the only time I ever observed any semblance of vanity in my husband.*

He taught chemistry for thirty-four years in the Keystone Oaks School District *and I taught in the same building as he so I knew how much the kids loved and respected him... year after year they would return during their freshman year of college to tell him how his teaching had helped them... kids who went to prestigious Ivy League universities like Princeton and Brown and Carnegie Mellon... together we chaperoned more dances, football games, and school gatherings than we could ever recount... when I began to coordinate a* *community service learning program he helped with every project, raking leaves for senior citizens and setting up lighting in the auditorium for the Teddy Bear Holiday, even surprising me with a shirt that said Mama Bear on the back, a gift he gave to me the day of the program...so often he came to my defense whenever I had been unjustly criticized yet he always let me know privately, in no uncertain terms, when I had crossed the line and was at fault for some untoward incident that had happened in school.*

Surviving are his wife Carol *who is barely able to function on her own after forty-four years of having this man in her life... the woman who is so wretchedly lost that she doesn't know if she will ever find her way out of this cataclysm and often doesn't care and wonders when the tears will stop and some kind of calm will finally descend upon her,* **daughter Jennifer** *the first-born child whose father recognized her early predisposition to car sickness because he suffered motion sickness himself and knew when she was going to be sick... a child who reveled in the adoration that only a loving Daddy could convey when he came flying into the house every day after school and asked where Daddy's big girl was... the teenager that the father taught to drive, thereby cultivating her love for stick-shift automobiles... the young woman whose father walked her down the aisle and later proudly declared that his harem had been extended when she produced her first daughter... the woman whose father who made her very happy because he treated her husband as a son rather than a son-in-law... the child-woman who had to say her goodbye early to a father she loved with all her heart because her own small children needed her back in South Carolina,* **and Stephanie** *the second daughter who always walked to a different drumbeat and yet knew her Dad was just fine with* *that... the teen who wept when her father knocked on the bathroom door the morning, after a verbal duel the night before, to say he was sorry, and she knew that he rarely had to apologize for anything... the young woman who drove seventy miles to bring her father ice cream and balloons for his birthday along with her love and not- so- well-hidden concern about the recent diagnosis of leukemia... the woman who declared that if she ever has a son he would be named Noel because no other name could be considered.*

He was preceded in death by his father, *a generous man whose kindheartedness was reflected in his son... a man who made the deceased's wife feel at home when the teenagers first dated... the one who came to the couple's efficiency apartment to stay for three days so he could paint their new home before they moved in and whose snoring during that time drove the young bride to the closet to sleep, causing the couple to laugh for months thereafter.*

No one is in charge because if someone were, this would never have happened. Lives would not have been torn apart by the loss of an individual who gave so much of himself and expected little or nothing in return. His remains are the ashes that reside in a simple mahogany box beside a picture of the couple taken in Mexico a decade before when life was defined by funny hats, tropical drinks, and a parrot perched on the deceased's finger. And by the way, when Noel John Lucas passed away at 60 years of age, sadly *he* was part of God's quota for that month.

SEVEN

ashes to ashes

Into the wind's breath and the hands of
the Star-maker we let you go.
-Ruth Burgess: "Saying Goodbye"

I have tried to convey the difficulty a widow encounters when she composes her husband's obituary. I could never have asked anyone else to do this for me; the words had to be mine, and as sterile as those words might have appeared in our small-town newspaper, it was *my* effort to pay tribute to my husband. Equally difficult was deciding how Noel's ashes would be handled, and eventually this became a task for others as well as for me. After Stephanie identified her father's body, we were told there would be a waiting period of four to five hours; of course I realized this was the time needed for the ashes to cool, something I chose not to think about. I have little recollection of how we spent that time; I remember we tried to have lunch but soon accepted neither of us was hungry. When we returned to the crematorium, we were given multiple copies of Noel's death certificate and advised of the number of places that might require proof that the man we loved was no longer with us...as if a piece of paper could prove more than our hurting hearts were telling us.

Then we were handed a box; I'm not sure what I expected or even if I had thought about the physical remains of my husband. I do know that while we had been waiting, it occurred to me that I was so grateful Noel and I had discussed cremation years ago. I was in an unfamiliar city with no idea how I would have arranged to have his body transported, much less *where* I would have taken him. We were two and a half years into our new life in South Carolina and did not have a burial plot there. Nor did we have one in Pittsburgh or either of the towns in which we had been born. Years ago when we turned our thoughts to this topic, it was assumed that would be a decision determined very far into the future, a mistake many make. But one thing was certain: Noel insisted he be cremated when the time came. I remember his joking about it, saying, "Don't you dare put me in a casket and let people come and gawk at me. Some fool is bound to say I look good, and then I'll have to sit up and tell him if he thinks I look good now, what the hell did I look like before, when I was alive?" That was when discussion of death was nothing more than dark humor. So now what I had left of my husband was encased in a gray plastic box, innocuous and heavier than I anticipated, if indeed I had any thoughts about weight or composition.

I have recounted the stop Stephanie and I made the first night in North Carolina, and our taking the ashes into the motel with us. Once I finally got Noel's remains back to our home, I didn't have the stamina or the courage to think about where these would be distributed. I took the box into our bedroom, and they remained in my closet for a couple of months. While immediacy wasn't as crucial as that of the publication of his obituary, I knew I had to address the issue sooner rather than later. Of course, a month after his passing was when I began to experience the messages he was sending, and dealing with those occurrences consumed me totally. Finally, I began to think about the many places Noel enjoyed as well as those people in the family who might want a small part of the man who was important to them. Once I set my mind to it, the ideas began to multiply, and what follows is the plan that made my husband a well-traveled man, even after he was gone from this earth.

When I finally decided to open the gray box, I admit to apprehension. I'm not sure what I expected, but much like Stephanie when she went in to identify her dad's body in Baltimore, I became a little giddy with the thoughts of what I might encounter. Of course, nothing occurred, and I set about filling containers with his ashes. Ironically, I used small test tubes with corks...I know my chemist husband would have approved. Earlier in the week I had gone to downtown Beaufort in search of a small carved wooden box, something fit to house some of Noel's remains. I devoted every bit of love and energy to that task, just as I would have for anything I may have purchased for him. After looking in several stores, I found exactly what I wanted. As the woman wrapped the finely crafted box, she asked, innocently enough, "What do you plan to use this for?" I limited myself to a brief smile and told her. The look on her face might generously be described as one of surprise although shock is probably more accurate. Then she regained her composure and indicated she hoped I would be pleased with my choice. I can imagine how the story played out when she repeated it. Furthermore, I don't have to use much imagination to know Noel's reaction for he surely was observing this from afar, and I'm sure his sense of humor was firmly in place.

Of course I made sure each of Noel's sisters, as well as his mother, received some of his ashes. At the time his younger sister and her husband were resettling in New Mexico, and I asked her whether or not she would be willing to take some of his remains out into the desert and scatter them. Knowing how he had enjoyed our trip there and feeling an affinity for that spiritual part of the country myself, I was certain Noel would approve. She wrote to me and told me she had scattered them well out in the countryside and said a few words to him as she did so. Reading her letter, I knew this was a good decision.

One of my husband's favorite pastimes was fishing, and it suited his laid back personality. For years he and some of his fellow teachers went to Canada in the summer to fish for a week. They would return grubby, bearded, and totally satisfied with their manly adventure. I was never comfortable being alone for that week, but I also recognized his need to get away with the guys. Thus it seemed reasonable to inquire whether or not these friends still continued their yearly trek, and if so, might they be willing to take some of Noel's ashes to the lake he loved so much. The answer was an affirmative, and the actual dedication was probably as ribald as they were when they all convened there in years past. That part was never disclosed to me, rightly so, but I am so grateful that became one more place where my husband came to rest.

There were places around home that fascinated Noel, and one he stopped to visit repeatedly was the Old Sheldon Church near Yemassee. This is an abandoned structure that dates back to the Revolutionary War, and my husband loved to wander among the tombstones and absorb the history they convey. Noel had often commented that he should make inquiries to see if there might be an historical society that tends to these grounds, adding that he would be interested in joining. This was another spot where I took some of my husband's ashes on a sunny afternoon when I was less emotional and more focused on my mission to honor Noel to the best of my ability.

Knowing there would be no burial with an accompanying headstone for my husband, I chose, instead, to have a gathering at my home to celebrate his life. Part of this included the placing of a bench on the fourth hole of our home golf course, a par three where the tee shot crosses the water. This hole happens to face the direction of our house which is situated on the first fairway. Noel loved that hole, and so with permission from the course owners, I was able to place a beautiful teak bench, hand crafted by one of Noel's golfing friends, at that tee. Attached was a bronze plate that stated: In memory of Noel John Lucas, husband, father, grandfather, friend and golfer. One of my girls suggested that perhaps the golfer status should have been moved up in line, knowing their dad's love of the sport. Of course, some of his ashes were scattered around that bench. When we dedicated the bench, I told the men with whom he golfed, "Know that he will smile when your tee shot lands on the green; know also that he will laugh when you miss it."

There is a magnificent live oak that grows behind our home. When we purchased the lot, we speculated then that it must be at least a hundred years old, and that tree was a large part of deciding where we would build. I came to refer to it as 'Noel's tree'. I wanted a lot on the water while he wanted the lot with *the tree*. I said, "If we buy your lot, then I get the house plan I want." It was only proper then that some of his remains came to rest under his tree.

Finally there was the evening Stephanie and I sat on the porch, and our conversation turned to spreading her dad's ashes. We discussed the many places his remains had been sent, and we got around to his love of the water surrounding us. Suddenly, my daughter said, "Why not put some of them in the Beaufort River? We can take the golf cart onto Vivian's Island and access the dock there." And so we got one of the containers, and as we were going out of the driveway, Stephanie said, "Wait a minute...go back to the house." When I inquired why, she responded, "You'll see." I hit the garage opener, and she went directly to the refrigerator in the garage that Noel had designated as his. When she emerged, she had a beer in her hand, and she was laughing. "You don't think Dad would want to be out on the water without a beer, do you?" I let my daughter take charge of this dedication, and as I observed her walk down to the end of the dock and scatter the ashes, followed by the can of beer, I felt Noel must surely be watching our child as well, amused at her sense of humor as well as her knowledge of him. She had always been, was at that moment, and still is her father's daughter!

As I made my way through those first months of loss, decisions like the ones I have recounted here actually helped me, and they gave purpose and some structure to an otherwise confusing and untenable situation. My goal back then was to think about the good times my husband had enjoyed and to use those is a positive way. To work diligently toward that goal was most assuredly a positive step in what was the beginning of my long, continuing trek.

EIGHT

the way we were

He who has gone, so we but cherish
his memory, abides with us,
more potent, nay more present than the living man.
-Antione de Saint-Exupery

In the days and months immediately following the passing of a loved one, there is never a time you are permitted to forget, even momentarily, what you have lost. The well of reminders is without a bottom, and those reminders can be gut-wrenching. If I think about the number of occasions when I was reduced to sobbing by something that would have seemed trivial under other circumstances, it is amazing I could hold myself together long enough to go out and retrieve the newspaper from the driveway. I found I began to mentally categorize everything I saw and experienced as pre or post Noel's passing. Old magazines I might pick up that had been published in the late nineties, or an outfit I wore that I knew he had liked brought about the recurring thought, "This was back when times were so good."

Feeling drained one day after a lengthy and debilitating round of tears, I had what most would agree was a curious thought. As I sat dabbing my eyes and wiping my nose, an idea dropped unsolicited into my brain: I wonder how David Letterman might approach widowhood in his famous Top Ten routine. Talk about dark humor! For some reason I forced myself to sit down at that moment and construct a list of times when the painful reminders had numbed me beyond much ability to reason. What follows are the musings that emerged from the seriously odd collaboration with myself. I am certain all widows have had similar experiences, and I'm just as sure each woman can provide equally stunning examples that have stopped her cold. While I recognize Letterman's lists are intended to be humorous, I have, nevertheless, borrowed his format for something very subdued, and thus offer the top ten situations when you know you have lost someone important, someone you love so much, someone you won't see again on this earth.

#10: You go into a department store, and, invariably, you enter the door leading directly to the men's clothing department. You leave in tears because every nerve ending tells you to do what you have always done before- pick out a great shirt and a pair of pants you know he will like.

#9: You see a man and woman together in a restaurant, and if he were to take her on the table right then and there, it wouldn't necessarily affect you. However, he simply places his hand at the small of her back as he opens the door for them to exit, and this leaves you motionless. How often did your husband do the same without thinking, making it such an intimate gesture?

#8: You see a commercial on television that shows an older man with his granddaughter. The love that each has for the other is so apparent. You know your own granddaughter feels the loss, because she often says that she hopes her Pop Pop is happy in heaven, and you feel the depth of her sadness.

#7: You come upon something he has written, and the familiarity of his penmanship stuns you. You don't want to throw away any evidences of his writing, because it is physical proof he was with you; it is more poignant, perhaps, than a photo.

#6: Something funny happens that you know will amuse him, and for one millisecond you can't wait to share it with him and hear his rich bass chuckle.

#5: You see a man sitting on a bench in the mall, and you instinctively realize he is waiting for his wife. How many cumulative hours did your understanding husband wait while you shopped idly? You wish you could regain even a small portion of the lost time, vowing you wouldn't make him wait.

#4: The mail that comes to you is wrong regardless of how it is addressed. Those pieces that have always been sent to both of you now arrive with only your name, a blatant reminder of just how alone you are. Equally upsetting are the envelopes that come addressed to both of you. Shouldn't everyone know what has happened and recognize the sadness that now consumes your life?

#3: The first time you put the lights on the Christmas tree by yourself, one strand promptly goes out when the last one is connected. You used to whine that the tree needed more lights. Now you know why he stood his ground on this annual argument, and you cry at your selfishness.

#2: You rummage through his toolbox, trying to find a particular tool to do a job you can't do anyway, so why are you bothering? In your search, you come across an old pair of his shorts that he used as a rag, and you dissolve into tears.

And finally, the number one way you know you are widowed:

You decide it is all right to wear your lacy black underwear to go out one evening. However, when you return home, wistfulness overrides any fun you might have enjoyed earlier as you remove your bra and panties yourself, knowing how it used to be when he was there to do it for you.

The occasions when these memories drop in unannounced are profoundly sad. The reminders will always be there, but over time the pain does diminish. It used to be when I emerged from those periods of despair, I felt my life was much like a document that had been relegated to a paper shredder: the pieces were still there, but there was no discernible 'whole' to be recognized. Later, I began to accept that as we widows reinvent ourselves, it is necessary to engage in the tedious process of collecting those pieces, using some, discarding others, but ultimately putting together what remains to form a 'new whole' that works for us now. There are memories among those pieces, and I *want* to remember the times that made my life with Noel so good; I *want* to integrate them into my new life and make them part of the different rhythm that now pulsates within me; I *want* to keep them with me throughout the remainder of my time on earth, and as my life moves forward, they may rest upon some back shelf of my consciousness, but at least they will be accessible. If I can rekindle these memories, and care for them much as one might tend a small fire, surely they will serve me well. It is Mitch Albom who provides words of reassurance in his poignant novel, *The Five People You Meet in Heaven*. His main character, Eddie, is a crusty old man whose last deed on earth is saving a child in an amusement park accident. He is killed as a result and goes to heaven where he meets five people who impacted greatly upon his life. One is his wife, Marguerite who speaks so eloquently when she attempts to explain how love survives on the other side.

"Lost love is still love. It takes a different form, that's all. You can't see their smile or bring them food or tousle their hair or move them around the dance floor. But when those senses weaken, another heightens. Memory. Memory becomes your partner. You nurture it. You hold it. You dance with it. Life has to end, love doesn't."

For the most part, the entwining of my life with that of Noel has made me what I am today. The love he gave unconditionally over the forty-four years we were together has left indelible fingerprints on me, and while the memories of the way we were may produce sadness and longing, they also provide a map to guide me as I proceed on my journey through the remainder of my life. I hold steadfast to the notion that some place over there will permit my husband to place his hand on the small of my back once again. If shopping is permitted, and my memory serves me well, I won't make him wait one minute. And finally, the heaven I like to believe exists will definitely sanction black lingerie, especially if Noel has a vote.

NINE

rediscovering the spiritual path

I believe in the sun, even when it's not shining.
I believe in love, even when I don't feel it.
I believe in God, even when God is silent.
lyrics from "I Believe" by Mark A. Miller

The integrity of my story requires me to address spirituality head-on. After all I lean heavily on the concept throughout my book, so some explanation is called for. I recognize the meaning of what is spiritual, as well as the importance of that meaning, varies from one person to another. Even today, knowing I have attained what I deem to be a level of serenity far beyond anything I ever believed possible, I still find myself questioning how spirituality impacts my life. Of one thing I am certain, however; much of what has brought me to this time and place is grounded in my having been given glimpses of things I cannot logically explain. Furthermore, I find it unnecessary to lean upon the crutch of logic to hold onto my beliefs.

I do not adhere to organized religion. While my reasons are many, the strongest is what I perceive to be a prevailing hypocrisy that permeates so many organized groups. I am angered by the perversions I believe have been, and continue to be, committed in the name of religion, any religion. There are far too many who are content to simply "talk the talk." Furthermore, questions such as 'What would Jesus do?', or a two inch headline trumpeting, 'What would Jesus eat?', an introduction to gardening in the Biblical tradition that appeared one time in a local newspaper, are a turn- off to me. While I don't know the answer to either query, and I am willing to concede that those who seek such information might get it, whereas I don't, I feel fairly certain Jesus must be appalled by the fast and loose play with his name, and I am equally confident he would never have wanted to be the subject of a bumper sticker or a license plate. Some will see me as a cynic at best and a blasphemous heretic at worst; regardless, these are views I have held all of my adult life. A walk on the beach at dusk or standing among the looming trees in the mountains brings me closer to the God I believe in and to His universe than the four walls of a steepled building can accomplish on Sunday morning.

To keep my story honest, however, I think it is necessary to include one situation that flies in the face of what is, by all calculations, my aversion to organized religion. During the thirteen days Noel lay comatose, I spent almost every moment of the daylight hours in the hospital. Much of that time I was in his room. However, when I went to lunch, almost without fail, I would return by way of a large statue located in a stories-high rotunda in the hospital, a statue of Christ that must be at least twenty feet tall, or so it seemed.

I made it a point to sit near the imposing figure for a few minutes, and I know that I spoke to Him in my mind, although I don't recall any attempts to bargain for Noel's life. For some reason I was drawn there, and it is not an overstatement to say I was 'religious' about my daily visits to the greatest symbol of the Christian faith. I am the first to admit this speaks to what may be *my* hypocrisy. Or perhaps those visits are just one additional bit of proof there are no atheists (or even agnostics) in the foxholes of life. All I can say in my defense is I was pulled to the massive figure, and despite the flurry of activity coming into and departing the building through that entrance, those visits provided some sense of comfort to me when I really needed it.

Now is the time to emphasize that I am *neither* an atheist nor an agnostic, because my belief in a much higher power than I can imagine is unshakeable. Seeing the magnificence the world offers to us every day, I firmly believe these wonders do not occur through happenstance. I accept without question there was a Big Bang, but on a whole other level I like to think it was a delighted God clapping His hands over everything He had in mind for us at the beginning of time. For me evolution and creationism have never been mutually exclusive. Those who disbelieve in any greater entity will respond that perhaps I have failed to observe the madness, pain and injustice permeating the daily news. Yet I believe all of it, the good and the evil, are part of a plan much greater than any of us can comprehend. More times than I can recall, it was my faith in such goodness that sustained me when I was inconsolable during the first months after Noel's passing.

Trying to determine when my interest in the spiritual became more than just idle curiosity is something I pondered many times after I lost my husband. It is easy to accept that my loss pushed me to search for *any* compelling explanation, but as I began my quest, I soon came to realize even before Noel's passing, there were times when unexplained forces had converged, and my need to explore and understand more about life after death and the soul's destiny had kicked in. At the time they were quiet blips on the screen that passed and were forgotten. But when I began to think more clearly, loss became my motivation and memory was my ally. And so I started to connect some of the dots. I began to see I wasn't making a grand discovery *because* Noel had passed away, something that would have upset me. Rather it was rediscovery of things I had observed earlier in my life and had either forgotten or dismissed as unimportant. His passing simply offered a magnification and subsequent fascination I hadn't experienced up till then.

During my college years, my close childhood friend, MD, became more open about spiritual encounters she had experienced, not only as a child but also as a grown woman. She has lived in the same house throughout her life and still resides there part-time. While not exactly frightening, these stories were sometimes unsettling. I often laughed and told her had I known as a child what was happening in her house, overnight stays would have been out of the question. Much of what she told me was interesting, and had I been focused on the larger picture, I might have paid closer attention. As it was, while I never doubted for a moment my friend's integrity when recounting these incidents, I tended to dismiss them, because I had never personally experienced anything of this nature. Seeing is, after all, believing, a concept that would ultimately, for me, be turned on its head.

In the spring of 1993 I attended a conference in Albuquerque, New Mexico, and while I was there I traveled with friends to Santa Fe, taking the old road north through the desert. It was a logical tourist's choice, nothing that would raise an eyebrow. However, I have come to accept there are few, if any, coincidences in life but rather a series of extraordinary events that eventually make sense, if only in retrospect. Thus, I tend to believe I was guided to that road for a purpose. Some use the word synchronicity or *meaningful* coincidence to describe these happenings. Even now, if I close my eyes, I can vividly see the starkly beautiful surroundings. At one point I asked my friend who was driving to stop the car; thinking I was ill, she quickly pulled to the side of the road. When I got out, my sense of awe held me momentarily immobile. Finally I snapped out of it and, turning three hundred sixty degrees, somehow recognized what I was observing and feeling was unlike anything I had ever experienced before. Furthermore, I felt certain I was *supposed* to be experiencing a revelation, although I couldn't have explained what was being revealed. When I returned home, I told Noel it had been a spiritual time but could not clearly articulate what I meant or what had happened to me during the brief stop.

The fall of 1996 brought me back to the Southwest for another conference. By that time Noel had retired, and I was in my last year of teaching with plans for my own retirement in the spring. At my insistence, he accompanied me, and before the conference began, we toured the area, visiting the Painted Desert, Monument Valley, the Grand Canyon, and yes, the road between Santa Fe and Albuquerque. A print reflecting the brooding spirit of the desert hangs in my home today, and I am certain now Noel and I were meant to experience the landscape together. His response may not have been as overtly intense as mine, but I know he was moved by what he saw.

Not long ago I looked through the journal I had kept on that trip, and one statement jumped off the page. Back then I wrote, "This part of the country shouts of the magnificence of God and the insignificance of man." That observation notwithstanding, I would like to be able to say those trips represented the beginning of an amazing awakening. However, in the months and years that followed, my life embraced nothing of such magnitude, and I would have to wait until my husband passed away to tap into the experiences that left me with the feeling I had been given a momentary look at another world. In many respects my trips to New Mexico were the infant steps of my spiritual trek, hesitant footfalls leading to the edge of somewhere in the loneliness of the desert. Just as I came to recognize I am not alone on my journey now, so do I believe my introduction almost a decade before to that serene vista was meant to be a resource I would store away, one that I could bring out later and examine many times in the months after my loss.

I have been told I am a strong woman, and I suppose it is true. I remember speaking at Noel's retirement luncheon, and the words came from my heart when I suggested that every man in the room needed to imagine bringing his wife to his workplace every day. "Furthermore," I said, "imagine your wife is assertive, frequently aggressive, and lord, sometimes abrasive as well. This is what Noel Lucas had to deal with during much of his working life." People in the room laughed, and many nodded knowingly, because I have always admitted to being a take-charge kind of person, sometimes with the not-so-desirable ramifications that term implies. Regardless of the manner in which I approached many issues with the resulting repercussions, there was always a constant in the equation, and that constant was Noel. He was my rock in any situation. To suddenly be without that support left me numb, and all the talk about my supposed strength and the ability to get through my grief became so much white noise. Yet, I did discover a toughness within myself I never knew existed, and I believe that strength was generated by my husband, wherever he might have been. Without reservation I am certain his spirit imbued within me the stamina I so desperately needed during those early months after his death. My husband's assertion decades before that I would get along better than I thought if he passed first proved to be fairly accurate. What he failed to say at the time, however, was that he would be there to help.

The first time I felt Noel was with me at home was three weeks after my return from Baltimore. It was Sunday, and I was sitting alone on our screened porch with my coffee and the newspaper. The morning was a pleasant one in early May, and the cloying heat of a typical Southern summer had yet to blanket the area. It was, however, very still. Our back yard has a number of trees, and when we moved into the house, Noel had deliberated where to hang a set of wonderful, throaty wind chimes my father had made for me shortly before he passed away in 1990. In Pittsburgh we had positioned them at a corner of the back deck that received a constant breeze, and when they chimed I would tell Noel it was my Dad talking to me, only half believing my conjecture then. In this yard I selected a tree where I thought they should be hung, but after a few weeks Noel noticed they weren't getting the wind, and he said he would have to move them elsewhere. The transfer never took place.

That May morning the chimes began to sound, and when I looked out, it appeared as though someone had gone by and given them a push. My first thought was there must be a good breeze despite my earlier observation, certainly one strong enough to set the chimes in motion. I looked up into the trees, but they were motionless. I continued to read, and the chimes sounded a second time, this time louder than before. Putting my paper down, I walked out into the yard. There was not a hint of air movement anywhere, and as I walked toward the trees, trying to determine whether or not the wind was gusting out there (it wasn't), the chimes abruptly became silent. Instinctively, I knew Noel was trying to let me know he was with me.

The following week was the one preceding Mother's Day. I was in the office, trying to give some semblance of order to my disorderly life, having filed several bills and papers. When the job was almost complete, I went downstairs. Several minutes later I returned to the room, and I noticed there was a notebook lying at the top of the steps that I had failed to put away. I didn't remember leaving it there, but then I was distracted most of the time, so this didn't strike me as unusual. I picked up the book and was about to put it away when a card fell to the floor, the front of the envelope staring up at me. Noel always wrote a simple C on the envelopes of all the cards he gave to me, and this one was no different. I couldn't imagine why a card would have been in the notebook as I tended to keep all of my cards from him together in one place; yet I was ready to believe this was an exception. I picked it up, and when I opened the card, it was a Mother's Day card he had given to me previously. Why in that notebook? Why a greeting card specific to the upcoming holiday, a time he had always made special every year from the time our daughters were born and long after they had moved out of the house? This was a man who consistently assured me I was a good mom to our daughters, and this year, as the card seemed to suggest, would be no different, despite his absence. These occurrences, as well as the powerful incident of the canceled checks appearing on the island kitchen, all converged to make me sufficiently aware of the need to stop and take note of what was happening. And so, one month after being pulled into an earthquake of loss I thought had shattered me forever, the aftershocks began, and how wonderful they were!

TEN

seeking my comfort zone

Walking with a friend in the dark is better
than walking alone in the light.
-Helen Keller

I need to make it clear that the messages I believed I was receiving from my husband, while both exhilarating and comforting, were also cause for me to ask myself whether or not I had slipped into periods of delusion. I acknowledge I am not necessarily an analytical thinker; yet I have always been smart enough to keep myself focused on the task at hand and work through problems with a fair degree of success. At this juncture I still possessed enough coherent thought to recognize the need to take a deep breath, step back, and try to assess what was happening to me. Was I so consumed by grief that I could no longer discern the difference between reality and fantasy? Noel and I had rarely discussed our beliefs on life after death; certainly we never came to any conclusions, implied or stated. Now I found myself wishing we had explored the topic together as I kept returning to the possibility I was actually receiving messages from him. Yet how does one make that determination when she is stuck in the middle of the greatest emotional crisis of her life? Fortunately, there was a person to whom I turned immediately for guidance as I tried to make sense of events that seemed to occur more and more frequently. This was my friend MD, who remained an integral part of my life right into our adulthood and is still very dear to me, despite the geography separating us. Indeed that closeness proved to be all the more precious when she hastened to assure me I was not losing my mind.

I have known MD since I was five years old. She is a year older, very feisty, very Irish, and as I came to find out in the years to come, very spiritually attuned. The night of April 8, several hours after Noel passed away, I spoke with her from Baltimore, and she assured me she had many reasons to believe Noel was fine and on the other side, and I should hold onto this. "I will see you soon," she said, "and I'll explain what happened here. Simply trust me right now." Strangely enough I was content to do so, and when I hung up the phone, a calm settled over me, something I never could have believed possible twenty-four hours earlier when my world had crashed and burned.

The next month my friend traveled from Pennsylvania to South Carolina to be with me, an act of generosity I will always remember with deep gratitude. She, Noel and I had been together from grade school through college. We were in one another's weddings, we had vacationed together, and our first born children even share the same birth date. That our lives continued to intertwine into adulthood seemed natural. Thus, when she first arrived, hours were spent revisiting a time decades ago when we seemed to have so much ahead of us. It was a time of much needed therapy for me, an occasion to speak of Noel and to cry without inhibition. As we sat on the porch throughout the warm evenings, drinking wine and talking into the early morning hours, MD shared with me the events that had happened to her the night Noel passed away, happenings that would provide insight and start to lend credibility to my own experiences. During those hushed conversations, my hope was nourished, and I tentatively dared to believe my husband was giving me comfort from the other side. What my friend told me during those conversations became the impetus for me to pick myself up and move forward. The train was waiting…I simply had to step on board.

One of the first incidents MD related occurred the last day of Noel's life. She began by saying, "The day was a difficult one for me despite the fact that it was my birthday. I was so uneasy, and while I knew Noel was still in the hospital, I didn't know how he was doing at that point. As the day unfolded, I paced throughout the house, feeling certain he was about to pass away but was hanging on to life because of you."

Twice my friend went to the phone to call me at the hospital but backed away each time, unsure of what she would say even if she were able to get through to me. When her son and daughter-in-law came to take her to dinner, she went reluctantly. MD paused here, her voice becoming quiet, and she said, "I was totally disconnected from the evening's celebration, distracted, feeling something was so seriously wrong that I finally asked that they take me home."

Her uneasiness continued into the early morning hours, and when she went to bed, she was unable to sleep. She concluded by saying, "The last time I looked at the clock around two forty-five, I felt then Noel was gone." In Baltimore, my husband had slipped away at two thirty.

When my friend told me this story, I wasn't upset but instead felt reassured by her words, as though this were another piece of the puzzle. My challenge was to assemble the pieces and put them together.

Even MD's arrival in Beaufort in May took on some very interesting aspects. I had stepped out of the house briefly before she came, and what happened during the half-hour of my absence is worth including here. She was scheduled to arrive sometime in the afternoon, and I had told her if I weren't there, she should go to the screened-in back porch and relax until I returned. My friend said she walked around the backyard for a time, enjoying the shade and the water garden, my last birthday gift from Noel. Although she couldn't identify what it was, something about coming onto the porch made her hesitant. Finally she did go in, and as she sat there on the swing, she remembered hearing in her mind the hymn *Touched by the Wings of an Angel*. When she told me this story, she mused, "Why I would think of that song? I haven't been in a church for over twelve years, and that is the last time and place I heard it." Then she said she simply knew Noel was there, and he was sitting in the rocking chair, always his choice of seats on the porch. This was a detail she had no way of knowing.

There are those people who come into your life for a limited period of time, and while they may have an impact for a short duration, they exit and are heard from rarely, if ever again. Such might have been the case when my philosophy professor, Frank Takei, entered my life for what could have been a single college semester. When he arrived on the campus of the small state school I was attending, I was about to move on to my junior year. The summer before, I had determined that if I took twenty credits one semester and twenty-one the next, I could graduate a semester early. Newly engaged, I had made marrying Noel my first priority, so this scheme held much appeal because then I could get married a year earlier than previously planned. Forget that such an overloaded schedule, followed by nine credits of summer school while in the midst of preparing for a wedding could produce untold anxiety. At twenty-one years of age, I ignored all of these arguments and plunged headlong into my classes, one of which was philosophy.

Frank had just completed his doctorate and was, at most, ten years older than his students. He had grown up in Hawaii, of Japanese descent, and he was single. For many of us attending a small western Pennsylvania college in the sixties, he was pure fascination, a man steeped in Eastern culture, teaching a subject that took us to places in our own psyche that were, up till then, unexplored. Several students, myself included, pursued further interaction with Frank outside of class, and while there was nothing romantic about our relationship, he and I forged a friendship that would last beyond college. Frank attended my wedding in August of 1963, but after I graduated the following January, nothing more coordinated than a yearly Christmas card kept us in touch. However, our older daughter, Jennifer, who decided to go to the college her father and I had attended, took her philosophy course from Dr. Franklin Takei, and so he and I were reunited. This serendipitous occasion resulted in a wonderful resurgence of our past relationship.

A part of my belief includes the notion that many things happen for a reason. This is not to say I think everything in our lives is predestined, nor do I believe for a moment we do away with the ability to make choices. Rather I like to think those choices are solely ours to embroider into the tapestry of our existence in the manner we see fit. In my mind one crucial aspect of that decision-making process lies with the people we encounter. We can elect to embrace individuals and keep them as a part of our lives, or we can move away from them as we continue on our life-journey. I kept in touch with Frank Takei over a period of forty years by choice, not necessarily a focused effort, but certainly a choice for which I would come to be as grateful as I am for the lifelong friendship of MD. Another decade after my daughter's graduation would pass before Frank and I reconnected once again. Ultimately this man would re-enter my life at a time when I had to probe for answers, digging deeper than I had ever dug into any subject Dr. Takei might have brought forth in his philosophy class.

When Noel was diagnosed in November of 1999, the Christmas letter I sent to our friends the next month reflected my turmoil. Frank responded to that letter, and in January I sent him a lengthy e-mail about the derailment my life seemed to be undergoing. It seemed like the natural thing to do because he was a friend who had often provided valued insights in the past. He did not disappoint me, and my former professor responded in true Socratic fashion, asking me questions that required introspection on my part and forcing me to take a hard critical look at my situation in an effort to find the courage I needed. To this day I am unsure of the precise content of our exchanges, but it was sufficiently calming to make me realize I had rediscovered someone who could help me deal with my fear. Our continuing dialogue over the next several months would provide a haven where I was able combat my anxiety, and later Frank was a source of inspiration to which I returned repeatedly.

What follows is a portion of his response through email communication when I wrote to tell him Noel had passed away: "Carol, the process of movement from grieving for the transition of a loved one to the next level of existence to that of a life of personal self-reliance is one that each individual has to carve out for him/her self with the help and guidance of loved ones who are on this plane of existence as well as those 'voices' that speak to us from the other side. If we have been involved in a loving relationship, then we are never alone. Go on talking with Noel, as I am sure you have been doing, and I am sure he speaks to you. Both of you need one another's comfort right now. You need to know he's all right, and he needs to know likewise for you. Both of you are now entering new phases of existence with all the concomitant anxieties, fears, and insecurities."

I cannot say with certainty that I fully processed my former teacher's words at the time, but again and again I would return to this communication and process what this man was trying to convey to me. I hadn't thought in terms of Noel's needing comfort or of his concern for me. But why wouldn't this be the case? My gentle, loving husband had always shown his concern for me in more ways than I could count. I believe Frank's words subconsciously penetrated the fog of sorrow that shrouded me, and eventually I came to accept I had to show Noel I was all right. He deserved nothing less. This would be no small task, and it would take weeks, months and perhaps years to bring this about. But just as it had been when he was alive, my husband would help me over the hurdles.

By June of 2001, two months after Noel's passing, the experiences of the wind chimes, the Mother's Day card, and the inexplicable appearance of the canceled checks were behind me, though not far from my conscious thoughts. Just as meaningful was MD's experience when she visited our home. I wrote to Frank about all of this, and he responded by asking whether or not I would like to visit him and his wife Shelley sometime that summer at their home in Lily Dale, New York. He had told me a few things about the town, namely that it is inhabited mainly by mediums and spiritualists. Somehow it seemed to me a visit with Frank in that setting was timely and appropriate, given my state of mind. Thus it was in July, 2001, I flew to Pittsburgh, stopping first to see my college roommate. Then I traveled north to spend time with MD before going on to Lily Dale. Three months had done very little to diminish the unsteadiness that had become a part of my life, but embarking on this trip felt so right and so exhilarating that I could never have considered canceling it for any reason.

It was natural to go first to my friend's home. Whenever I visit there, I am taken back to a time when life was uncomplicated. Furthermore, memories of the countless hours I spent in that setting as a child always seem to emerge and take over, eliminating any stress I might be experiencing. Those childhood memories wrap a protective shell around me, regardless of my age or current circumstances. The unexpected bonus of this trip was MD's agreement to accompany me to Lily Dale.

As an adult I listened to stories and later wondered if perhaps her house straddles a warp that crosses the dimensions of time. The first night I was there, I dreamed Noel made love to me, the kind of dream I had not experienced since returning home from Baltimore. The same night I encountered another nocturnal blip that might seem unimportant unless one accepts the notion dreams can contain messages, something I came to believe over the next few months. In this dream my friend and I were in her kitchen. I was sitting at the breakfast bar, and she was looking for a part of the coffee pot, complaining it should have been in a particular place but wasn't there now. The next morning, as I sat at this same spot, my friend started to make the morning coffee, but she could not find a needed part for the pot. I was dumbfounded! The scene played out exactly as I had dreamed it, even the words she used to express her disgust at the inability to lay her hands on the missing part. When I told her what I had seen in my sleep, she laughed and said I must be attuned to the vibrations around me and added this kind of happening is called dreaming the future. In *An Experiment with Time*, Professor JW Dunne proposes "all time that is now, has been, or ever will be is like a river, and you can navigate this river forward or backward in the vessel of your dreams." Because of the many dreams I experienced during the months and years following Noel's passing, I became fascinated with Dunne's concept and read several books on the topic. Belief in the significance of dreams has been a part of man's experience since the beginning of time, and this belief shows up in literary works, ranging from the Bible to Shakespeare. Over time television has broached the concept as well. *Medium's* Allison DuBois explored the dreamscape consistently, and a television series entitled *Fast Forward* dealt with the idea that everyone on earth, with few exceptions, managed to dream the future when they blacked out for a brief period. That my dream of the previous night was replayed in exact detail the next morning leads me to think there is validity in Dunne's concept. On that June morning, perhaps my dream was intended to be a precursor to the world I was about to enter.

And so, a few days later, MD and I drove north across the Pennsylvania state line into Lake Erie country and on to Lily Dale, New York. In some respects we may as well have plotted our course for Mars or the Land of Oz. Ironically my childhood friend and my former professor would come together with me in this small village, and this convergence would produce an event so profound that my life would be forever changed.

PART TWO

In order to get to the rainbow,
we must first conquer the rain.
-unknown

ELEVEN

arriving in lily dale, take one

All spiritual practice is the art of shifting perspective.
-Teal

L ily Dale is a small village, sixty miles south of Buffalo, New York, located a few miles out of Cassadaga, in Chataqua County. Upon first observation, some call the gated town quaint; others will counter with "other worldly" because it is said to be the world's oldest and largest spiritualist community. Many of the permanent residents are registered mediums, and thousands of visitors enter through the town's gates every year to engage the services of one or more of these individuals who are believed to channel spirits from the other side. Susan B. Anthony and Eleanor Roosevelt are among the dignitaries said to have visited this small hamlet often.

At no time when making plans to visit Lily Dale did I let myself dare to hope Noel would make a connection with me there. Some may find this strange, even unbelievable, but it is true. Of course there had been the occasions at home that had raised the possibility in my mind, but I wasn't on sure footing with those, given my blunted sense of reality. I simply could not risk setting myself up for bitter disappointment, so I told myself if I went without the baggage of a preconceived notion of what *might* happen, I could leave Lily Dale with any excuse that would make the failure of communication bearable. This was my way of retaining control, and somewhere in the dark cavern of my grief, I recognized any small amount of control was crucial.

MD and I arrived on a sunny afternoon and stopped to pick up our pass at the gate where there was a young man who ushered us on through to the land of enchantment. Thoughts of St. Peter skittered through my mind, but by the looks of this kid with his short haircut and boyish grin, he had a long way to go if he wanted to assume such a lofty position. Frank had called in the pass, and we followed his directions to the house although we didn't have far to go. One doesn't walk, much less drive, very far to reach any location in Lily Dale; it is a town meant to be idly strolled from one end to the other. My knowledge of the town's history was quite limited then, and I can say definitively I felt nothing ethereal when entering those gates. The pastel Victorian homes situated close to the narrow streets were simply a throwback to a period from the past. At the same time I thought about the number of small towns in America fitting into this mold. However, I would soon come to realize Lily Dale is not Americana as we think of it.

My reunion with Frank was an easy one. Although we hadn't seen one another for a decade, I was at once comfortable in his presence. His wife, Shelley, was sufficiently intuitive to give us some time alone so we might re-establish a connection, one rarely achieved through Christmas cards and emails only. She and MD moved to another part of the large house while Frank and I caught up, although it was apparent the often referred to 'elephant' was in the room as we talked. Frank began to tell me what I might encounter while visiting this admittedly eccentric village. He asked what I expected, and my answer was a quick and definitive, "Nothing." As the afternoon began to wane, Shelley returned to the room to ask whether or not I would like to go to the Forest Temple for the outdoor message service. Of course I would. I was, after all, here for every aspect of the experience; in for a dime, in for a dollar as they say. Later I would come to view that stroll on a warm July evening to the wooded glen close by as nothing short of the beginning of my enlightenment. It was a decision that would change not only how I would deal with my loss in the months and years to come, but also how I would view the world and the objectives that would come to govern my life from that point on.

We took a seat at the back, behind of a group of perhaps fifty people. Several mediums stood behind us, some of them permanent residents, others visitors to Lily Dale. As each was introduced and came to the front of the group, he or she scanned the expectant faces and finally settled upon one for whom a reading would be provided, if the person were willing to receive it. I cannot imagine anyone refusing this opportunity, but it is the etiquette of each medium to ask, "May I come to you?" I remember listening to these random readings with a kind of detachment, not letting myself hope one of these mystical figures might single me out to let me know Noel was near and willing to communicate. When the service ended, everyone wandered away, some cheerful, most contemplative. Mine was a combination of relief and disappointment.

We arrived back at the Takei home, and Frank, who had not gone with us, asked what I thought. I wasn't sure how to answer, but then what did I have as a basis for comparison? Some of the readings had been very poignant, one in particular. A heavy-set, blond medium, very pretty and possessing a beautifully modulated voice, sought out a gaunt woman sitting close to where I was seated. It was apparent that this woman was dealing with the ravages of chemotherapy, and she wore a baseball cap to cover her baldness. I didn't pay close attention to what the medium told her because my thoughts were racing, focused upon how horrific it would have been to see Noel in that condition. This was one of many times since his passing I was grateful he never had to undergo the pain and embarrassment that so often accompany cancer treatment. I mentioned this reading to the others, and Shelley said, "The medium who gave her the reading is Martie Hughes. We like her very much."

The evening wore on, and we finally went out to sit on the screened porch, enjoying some wine as well as the coolness that had settled upon the Dale. In the distance the quiet murmur of voices was punctuated with occasional laughter. At one point I looked up to see the screen door open, and a woman came onto the porch. Shelley started to laugh, and upon closer observation, I realized that it was the medium Shelly identified as Martie, the one we had seen earlier at the Forest Temple Service. Introductions were made, wine offered and refused, and finally she looked at me and said,

"You were at the Temple this evening. I would have come to you, but the woman I spoke to believes she has only a few weeks to live. I needed to make it clear to her that she has a few months to accomplish those things so important to her." Martie added that she hoped I would understand, and then she asked me the question I hadn't wanted to let myself think about. She said, "Do you want the message I received for you?"

We often read about the heart standing still, and while realistically we know that doesn't happen without dire consequences, there is a moment when we are motionless, no blinking of the eyes, no intake of breath. It was as though I had just come to the crest of the world's highest roller coaster plunge and was wondering how I got there. For a moment I believe my heart did pause a beat, and I whispered, "If you can give me a message, I would really appreciate it." What happened next can only be described as life altering.

TWELVE

the first encounter

All we're ever looking for is another open door.
-Kate Bush
English singer and song writer

Martie began her message with the declaration that Noel was a golfer, adding that he wanted me to know he had experienced two holes-in-one after his passing. My first emotion was one of panic, followed immediately by dejection. This was going to be some silly farce, full of affectation, with little meaning or significance. This woman was a friend of the Takeis, and yet she was going to treat lightly the subject that had tormented me for the past three months. I didn't know how I could stand it. Then she placed her hands on the table in front of her and said, "He says you still aren't standing correctly when you hit the ball. He is showing me this by use of his hands." With this comment she moved her right hand back a bit and said, "He says you are standing like this, and when you hit the ball, it goes off to the right, like this." She then moved her right hand in a curving motion, pantomiming a slice.

There was no mirror in which I could observe my face, but had I been able to do so, I'm sure my shock would have been apparent. During the countless times Noel and I had golfed together, he often tried to get me to change my stance before I hit the ball. When he did this, he never demonstrated with his feet but rather with his hands held out in front of him, moving his right hand back and swinging it to the right. My astonishment soon turned to ragged sobbing, because I knew only Noel could have conveyed this information to the woman sitting across from me. There is no way she could have guessed her way through this subject with such precise detail. I sat there and cried until I was spent, and in the wake of my emotional exhaustion, once more I felt serenity descend upon me, the likes of which I hadn't experienced since my talks with MD. Later Frank told me he had never witnessed anything like this reading in all the time he and Shelley had been coming to Lily Dale, and it was apparent they, as well as MD, were genuinely affected.

Martie next began to talk about the piles of papers she saw, saying it was evident that I had done a great deal of research during my husband's illness. This was true although the papers were no longer in piles but had been committed to three-ring binders. She continued, "Noel wants you to put this behind you now. Go home and tie the binders together with a red bow and put them in a box. You did all you could do."

Then she said something seemingly discordant, an incongruous detail, given the accuracy of the information she had provided up to this point. She stated simply, "Your husband passed quite a few months ago." I responded that it had been just three months, and that he had died on the eighth of April. She looked perplexed and said, "No, I am getting the sense he passed six to eight months ago." Given the reading I received the next day from a second medium, it will become apparent why this observation that appeared incorrect became important.

When I first decided I was going to visit Lily Dale, I asked Frank to recommend the medium he believed to be the most credible, and without pause or reservation he recommended Sherry Lee Caulkin, a medium who has earned a distinguished reputation within the community. Of course I took his recommendation to heart and made an appointment with Sherry Lee for the next day. However, after having talked with Martie Hughes the night before, I was almost tempted to cancel the appointment. How could I expect to gain any more than I had already received? Furthermore, if I were given conflicting information by Sherry Lee, would it taint the euphoria I was feeling on this beautiful sunny Saturday when all seem so right with the world? I didn't want to place Frank in the awkward position of having scheduled the reading only to have me decline at the last minute, so with this in mind, I walked across the street for my second encounter with the other side.

Frank and Shelley both emphasized that when they know a reading will be given, they provide no information about their friends to any of the mediums. Both are very sincere about this, and I believe them. Martie Hughes is a friend with whom they socialize, and later I had a chance to find out exactly what she knew about me prior to coming onto the porch that evening and delivering her message. She stressed she was aware I was widowed and a former student of Frank's. Other than this, she knew nothing of my background. Although Sherry Lee is a neighbor of the Takeis, she does not socialize with them. Frank and Shelley send friends to her because they believe she is highly thought of and very genuine.

Earlier Saturday morning I sat on the Takei's back porch, watching people come to and leave Sherry Lee's house. All appeared to be carrying a long roll of paper when they exited, and this stirred my curiosity. When I finally stepped onto her porch, I didn't knock on the closed door or ring the bell, but rather sat down and waited my turn. This was the procedure I had observed from my earlier vantage point; it was my sense that you didn't bang on the portal to the other side but rather waited to be summoned. A few minutes later a sweet looking blond woman of indeterminate age opened the door and welcomed me inside. The room to which she led me was comfortable, and nothing about the setting was intimidating. This could easily have been the home of any friend who had asked me to stop by for a cup of coffee.

Before going to my reading I had made up my mind I would provide as little information as possible, so I sat down quietly and began taking notes as soon as Sherry Lee started to speak, which was immediately. This is a woman who talks rapidly while drawing broad, sweeping, lines with chalk on paper as she speaks, thus explaining the rolls that were tucked under everyone's arm when each was leaving her house. "Your husband has passed to the spirit world," she said, sweeping her hand across the large sheet of white paper. "I sense bad blood: not an accident or an operation but *tainted* blood." I answered with the single word "leukemia."

"Your father has also passed, not your mother but your father. He was very instrumental in helping your husband across when he passed over. Your husband passed over several months ago." There it was again, the contention that Noel had died earlier than he did. I answered that it had been only three months, and Sherry Lee responded simply, "I think he should have passed before then, sometime between September and November, but I have the sense his father stepped forward to give him the necessary strength to ward off the danger. His father has also passed, has he not?" The words, while somewhat stilted, were said in a matter-of-fact way, and what she said was true.

At first, I was perplexed as to why two mediums within a span of twelve hours would insist Noel had passed away months before he did. Furthermore, both placed the time of his death in the fall of 2000. Later, when I got back to South Carolina, I looked through the binders that held Noel's medical records, specifically at the results of his blood tests. In November, his white count had spiked dangerously high, and we were certain he would have to begin treatment immediately. However, a week later another test showed a marked drop in his white cell count, and we figured we had dodged the bullet for the time being. In fact, the drop was fairly dramatic, a time for gratitude!

Sherry Lee continued the reading by saying Noel wanted me to know that he was very pleased with the gathering (her word) I had planned, that it was everything he could have wanted. She asked, "Does he mean his funeral?" I answered that it was a memorial service. She said, "Well, he says every detail was right." This pleased me because I had paid close attention to all aspects of the service that was held in our home, a gathering of friends and relatives who came to celebrate Noel's life.

Then she cocked her head, smiled ever so slightly and asserted, "You don't dream much of your husband, do you?" At this my eyes began to tear, and I said that I really wanted to but dreams of him just wouldn't come. Her smile broadened, and she replied, "Ah, but you had a dream recently, didn't you, and it was sexual. I see a sexual energy around you produced by that dream." I assume that my jaw dropped as I simply stared at this woman with wide eyes and an open mouth. While MD and I were walking together through Lily Dale the previous day, I had told her the bag of lavender she had placed on my pillow when I first arrived at her home had very potent power. I added that I had had wonderful sex with Noel in my dreams the first night in her house. We had laughed about it, and now here was Sherry Lee putting into words what no person other than my friend knew. My first thought was, "Good lord, this woman has the bushes bugged!"

You can imagine my friend's reaction later when I told her about this part of the reading. She who needs no persuasion regarding the reality of communication from the other side thought this was my idea of a joke. Not so, and I might add that three years later I was still sleeping with the same bag of lavender. Today it looks much like the well-worn, ratty plush animal a child might carry off to bed for nightly comfort.

Sherry Lee's reading continued, and it included an incident I hadn't given any thought to since making the long, tortured journey from Baltimore back to South Carolina three months before. She started by saying she believes everyone has a guardian angel, something I also believe although after Noel's death I tended to think mine must have abandoned me entirely. She continued with the reading, saying she saw my angel wearing what she first thought was a sash but upon closer inspection appeared to be a tire. I started to laugh and said that only my angel would be tacky enough to wear a tire. Sherry Lee didn't seem particularly amused by my observation and replied that the tire was meaningful. Had I been involved in an accident in which a tire blew out? This was apparently the feeling she was getting, and she insisted I think about the possibility when I had a chance. Well, I should certainly know whether or not I had been involved in an auto accident, and my only thought was to hope this medium wasn't looking into the future.

It wasn't until the predawn hours a day later that any of this made sense to me. I was back at MD's home, sleeping in the same bed in which Noel and I had connected a few days before. Suddenly I awoke and sat upright. The tire! I knew what Sherry Lee had seen! The revelation couldn't have been more profound had the Mormon Tabernacle Choir gathered around my bed with a musical explanation. When Stephanie and I were making our way back to South Carolina after having obtained Noel's ashes, I noticed what I thought was a shimmy of the car at the right front. What I know about auto mechanics can be placed in a thimble, and there is still room for my finger- in other words, nothing. Add to this my mental state, and very simply, I continued to drive blindly, southbound, not feeling much but annoyance about the wobble. Stephanie commented about it when she drove, and I responded that we would have my son-in-law, David, look at it when we got to their home, which I did.

He took the car around the block, looked at the right front tire and pronounced it bad enough to need replacement. He told me, when he returned from the garage, that the mechanic who changed the tire said to him, "I sure hope whoever was driving on this didn't go far because this thing is a bad accident waiting to happen." So my guardian angel hadn't abandoned me, and God love her, she protected my daughter as well. If she chose to wear a tire, that was perfectly fine with me.

Thus it was that I left Lily Dale that Saturday afternoon with thoughts tumbling through my brain at a pace similar to that of a load of clothes in a dryer. Neither MD nor I talked much during the first fifty miles of the return trip, but when we did begin to converse, we couldn't stop. The words fell over one another, and we couldn't get them out fast enough. How important was our visit to the Forest Temple? What did my friend remember about Martie's reading on the back porch? Should I believe these past few days represented nothing more than my wishful thinking? I knew I trusted Frank implicitly, but might he have said anything to either medium that permitted them to hit so close to home? My friend and I had come away from Lily Dale with perceptions that cried out for explanation. For MD, I am sure the events were an affirmation of much that she already felt to be true. For me, it wasn't quite that simple. I had to rid my mind of skepticism before I could begin to evaluate what had happened. This was the first step of a journey where I would search not only for explanations regarding so many aspects of my loss, but also for answers about my life in general and how I was going to move forward after my experiences.

THIRTEEN

the healing will begin

If you just set people in motion, they'll heal themselves.
-Gabrielle Roth

The first time a widow makes a conscious decision to move forward and try to climb out of the pit of despair into which she has been thrown, some rather astonishing empowerment takes place. Regardless of how slight her progress may seem, momentum is established, and the act takes on a life of its own. After spending those days in Lily Dale, during which time I made discoveries that at once baffled and comforted me, I knew I had to get myself to a quiet place and reflect upon everything I had experienced. Fortunately, I am a strong proponent of documentation and had kept a journal of my time there. Unfortunately, words on paper rarely reflect the powerful emotions arising from such encounters, and so I found myself doggedly seeking confirmation of what I *thought* I had experienced. Over the next few months I revisited everyone who had shared that hour on the Takei porch. What questions had Martie asked, and how, specifically, had I responded? As I came away from each inquiry with affirmations of what my own memory had already told me repeatedly, I began to accept that in as much as something rather extraordinary had happened, I needed to stop my persistent excavation and begin trusting my gut.

The trip to Lily Dale had produced hope and exhilaration I believed would never be mine again. That is not to say after my return to South Carolina my life was miraculously full of promise. Unexpected crying jags may have become fewer in number; nevertheless, they were still very much a part of my life. I wanted so much to use wisely the information I had been given by both mediums as I began my inquiry into what I prayed was real and true. To process these experiences in a rational way while I was still grieving seemed almost impossible. Often when I sat in the evening hours trying to mentally construct the plus and minus columns of my life, I felt as though I were attempting to reconcile magic with logic. A door that seemingly connected me with my deceased husband beckoned; yet I knew I still had to keep at least one foot firmly grounded in this world.

I soon began to feel like the child who chases fireflies on a warm summer evening, finally catching one of the amazing creatures in flight. She gazes at it through the glass jar, and with an innocent intensity, tries to discern exactly what she has within her grasp. In the light of day, the firefly is rather unremarkable, but now in the hours of pending darkness, it becomes something magical, as though a spell has been cast, allowing this insect to become a beacon as it emits a pulsating glow from within. The child doesn't know what entomology is at work, but she doesn't have to understand the details. I had been fortunate to capture the essence of some kind of mysticism while in Lily Dale, and it provided light for my darker moments. Why was it necessary I know how that light came about? Recently I stumbled upon a Biblical quote I wish I had seen back then. Hebrews 11: 1-3 states: "Faith is the substance of things hoped for and the evidence of things unseen." The complexity of my dilemma in trying to determine what was real in my Lily Dale experience was rendered rather simple in the light of this quote.

Eventually I came to accept it was all right to let the magic carry me forward. In doing so, I wasn't negating reality; rather I was simply choosing another path to the truth. Or so I told myself as I waged my on-going battle against letting despair take over. Before long I began to back away from using the word death, because I came to disbelieve that Noel had died. The Lily Dale readings as well as several books on the subject of afterlife brought me to another conclusion: I began to accept my husband completed the time he was allotted, or perhaps chose, here in this earthly classroom. It took me some time and a great deal of introspection to arrive at this decision, but when I did, I began to feel lighter, less burdened, as though I were gaining firmer footing in my new life. Furthermore, my verbalizing of this was also altered. Instead of using the word 'died', I found myself using phrases like 'passed away' or 'moved on.' To state that Noel died was no longer compatible with what I had come to believe happened that night in the hospital. His earthly body died, but I do believe very strongly his soul lives on.

I would occasionally engage in mind chatter (read this to mean a pity session) regarding Noel's transition, and I recognized my selfishness because it did not include me.

However, when I found myself navigating the marshes of depression and disappointment I sometimes wandered into, it was my younger daughter who tactfully pointed out, "It's not entirely about you, Mom." There is difficulty getting past this honest observation, but she was and still is right. I must trust I am exactly where I'm supposed to be at this time in my life, and Noel's work here was complete, thereby necessitating his moving on. I might not like it, but I believe my learning to cope with profound loss is part of a bigger plan, "my contract" as Carolyn Myss suggests in her book *Sacred Contracts*. After all, it is easy to be euphoric as you dance through the blissful times; it is a great deal more difficult to plod through dismal days, feeling there is little to keep you moving forward.

The moment I understood *and accepted* I was no longer coping with Noel's death, but rather I was dealing with his moving on, my healing required considerably less effort. One way to look at the loss of a loved one is to recognize and appreciate God loaned to you, for the briefest time, a treasure of immeasurable worth. Do you cry because you have to return the treasure? Probably, and that is all right. Nevertheless, a loan is just that, something temporary. You also need to focus upon how fortunate you were to be part of the transaction and try to move past the notion that you were cheated. I found if you can get to a place where the gratitude for what you had outweighs the pain of what you have lost, you are well on your way to moving forward with a cloak of serenity around your shoulders. Remember the oversized coat I spoke of earlier? The fit does become better.

When I was in Lily Dale the first time, Frank mentioned I had missed meeting Christine Wicker, a published author who had come there earlier with the intent of writing a book about the village that held me so entranced. He told me a bit about Christine, but in truth the information meant little to me then, and I forgot about her shortly thereafter. However, a couple of months later, when I was back in South Carolina, Frank called and asked whether or not I would agree to talk with Christine about her new project. I saw no reason to deny this request since I was still on a high from my experiences in the Dale. Furthermore, continuing events, most specifically the discovery of those missing checks, had convinced me more than ever that Noel was still around, and he was letting me know it. Any additional investigation into this possibility would be more than welcome.

The first call from Christine lasted over an hour, and I found I was exhausted at the conclusion of our conversation. Nevertheless I had a genuine sense of excitement, a feeling my life was undergoing still one more important shift. This phone call and those that followed in the weeks to come became 'couch sessions' in which I was given the opportunity to articulate my grief. Christine asked pointed questions, framed in such a way that I had to dig deep within myself for the answers. Yet, she was never the brash journalist who cornered the victim to talk about what it was like to view death (and possible afterlife) up close and personal. I wanted so much to articulate correctly what I had experienced, because I knew it was crucial, not only to the authenticity of her book but also to my understanding of what was real about the events that had left me with so many questions.

I poured my heart out to this woman whom I had never met, fully confident she would not make a mockery of my trust or question my pain. I am sure during these sessions I must have cried, although I recall very few specifics of our conversations. It seems odd to say, but I had to wait for the publication of Christine's book to fully appreciate how completely I had entrusted my most excruciating moments to a total stranger. And yet, at no time did the process feel anything but right.

In the fall of 2001, five months after having returned from my first visit to Lily Dale, I went to Raleigh, North Carolina to meet with Christine Wicker as well as two other women she was interviewing; all of our stories were to be part of her book *Lily Dale: the True Story of the Town that Talks to the Dead.* We gathered at the home where the Takeis reside most of the year, and as I drove north, a heady mix of excitement and apprehension overtook me. Would this experience pale in comparison to those of Lily Dale? Even worse, would the Lily Dale encounter somehow lose meaning when I came together with the others? Perhaps the other-worldly effect had evaporated like so much pixie dust, and I would find myself doubting all that had brought me to the point of what I considered my self-discovery. I need not have worried; like an intricate work of origami that is folded and refolded, this trip provided still another dimension of what I know is my journey.

The weekend in North Carolina was one of introspection. The Takei house sits on a lake in a heavily populated residential section of the city, something rare and delightful. Shelley has transformed their home into an Asian retreat with a splash of Lily Dale fairy-kingdom. My room was quiet and comfortable, almost like a cocoon, and I slept well during the time I was there. Frank had built a multilevel wood deck overlooking the lake, and as we all sat out there savoring the warmth autumn had saved for our pleasure that early November day, I remember thinking this was another spiritual encounter for me. The complete relaxation I felt was assuredly enhanced by my interaction with people who shared stories of reconnection with someone they had loved and lost. Their feelings reflected many of my own, and I was in awe to be in an environment where daring to believe in communication from those who had passed was shared by all because they had actually experienced it.

We exchanged stories, and as I listened to the others, I came to realize my experiences were not cruel fabrication, a subconscious conjuring I had let play havoc with my mind. While some might say this was a gathering of bereft souls seeking to commiserate with one another, I recognized there was much more to the meeting than I had imagined possible. During one of our many discussions, I offered up the idea that I was still fragile enough to believe what I had experienced was smoke and mirrors, and in some respects I was waiting for the painful, yet inevitable, reality to surface. One woman responded emphatically, "That isn't about to happen, not from where I'm sitting."

Probably the high point of this trip was finally coming face to face with the voice at the other end of the telephone. Christine Wicker is a poised, soft-spoken woman, pretty and very open to those around her. While she exudes charm, she is also very capable of getting the information she believes is necessary for her story. There is nothing pushy in her approach; instead she is tactfully methodical, often restating a question before she is satisfied that she has the sought-after exactness. "When you saw the checks on your kitchen island, do you remember exactly what you thought?" *Oh, my*

God, am I hallucinating? "How long do you think the wind chimes continued to ring before you started down your porch steps to check them out?" *Till the time I was within three feet of them.* Her delving caused me to reach deeper into the encounters with Noel than I had done before.

In the months following, I would have the opportunity to spend time alone with Christine, once when she flew into Atlanta, and again when she visited my home. When her book about Lily Dale was published, I came to appreciate the magnitude of what she had been able to bring about in me by providing the opportunity to tell my story. It is almost surreal to see your name in print in a hardcover book and to read the story you know so intimately, told in such a way that the truth seems carved in stone. I believe Christine Wicker is one more person who was placed in my path, someone who helped me see beyond the waves of sadness that often washed over me; it was she who provided a means by which I was able to set my sails for calmer waters.

I spent three days with the people who convened in Raleigh. The Takeis had been there when I experienced my first encounter with Martie Hughes in Lily Dale. They knew and understood the spontaneity of that moment and its impact upon me. Providing the reinforcement I needed after such an unsettling encounter, they deftly handed me over to Christine. She listened to my story over a period of weeks and tended to my sorrow with such sensitivity and kindness that I could talk freely about my loss. Finally, during this weekend I met with strangers who had no personal investment in my pain. Their own hurt was burden enough to bear, and yet they set aside momentarily the grief they were carrying to help me with mine. In a span of three days all of us seemed to meld into one entity whose sole purpose was to learn more about connecting with a world that was foreign to us. It was a time when I threw away caution and fear, and I opened my heart and mind to strangers, not caring if I appeared delusional or irrational. I allowed myself to trust these women; their stories were every bit as authentic as mine and their pain just as tangible. We would never have sought the circumstances that brought us together, but finding ourselves to be members of this ungodly sorority, we recognized the collective need to bond...and we did. Thus I left North Carolina in November of 2001 with one more part of my blueprint for healing clutched to my heart.

FOURTEEN

it's okay to laugh, even uproariously

Take time to laugh; it's the music of the soul.
A merry heart doeth good like a medicine,
but a broken spirit drieth the bones.
Proverbs 17:22

A widow cannot exist solely within the confines of grief and expect to be anything but dysfunctional. Without seeking some respite from our unhappiness, we will simply wither and turn inward. In spite of our sadness, we must hold fast to the reality that laughter is, indeed, medicine for the soul. Research has shown that those who are gravely ill often recover from their illness when their lifestyle includes a daily dose of mirth. Can it be any different with sickness of the heart brought on by widowhood?

Frank and Ernest, two comic strip characters, sometimes make very good sense. One time I smiled when Ernest asked, "Do you ever wonder about the grand scheme of things?" and Frank responded, "No, I have enough trouble with the daily subplots." Right after Noel passed away I felt that the bigger picture of my life had been greatly compromised, thus creating a huge void that left me dealing with an array of chaotic feelings, not the least of which was inadequacy. Mundane tasks took on new difficulty because those very chores had always included his input. Getting rid of the garbage became a crisis. Despite the bedlam, however, there were times of humor, and I am convinced that in the situation I am about to relate Noel laughed hardest from his observation post on the other side.

One morning shortly after I had returned from Baltimore, I was preparing the coffee, something my husband always did. He simply made much better coffee than I do, and I was content to let him do it. He always ground the beans fresh, and I determined I would do no less. This particular morning I pushed down hard on the grinder, and as I lifted my hand, the cap stuck to my palm while the grinder was still operating on high speed. Of course the result was ground coffee everywhere. I cried, I swore, and then I laughed, hysterically! That was the first of many situations where my lame attempts to do what he had completed with total ease promoted a smile that often turned to audible laughter. I got to the point where I simply looked up and told him I hoped my comedic frailties provided him with entertainment.

Noel chose to laugh so much of the time. I say 'chose' because there were issues in his life that could have brought about bitterness in him, but he never went down that road. Even when he was told he had leukemia and it was incurable, he did not dwell on his health, but rather lived the remainder of his life looking for the positive and laughing when the occasion was humorous. This was his approach to life for as long as I had known him. Often I saw the glass as half empty; Noel, on the other hand, chose to see it as half full, and when a situation was especially funny, no one came forth with a greater belly laugh than my husband. The recognition that I should take a page from his book if I were to get my life back on track came during my first brush with the other side in Lily Dale. When Martie Hughes came onto the porch, and the impromptu encounter ensued, I was a train wreck. When I had finished sobbing, she smiled and said, "He says not to cry because he likes it better when you are laughing." I made every attempt to regain my composure because I knew this to be true.

Sometimes when I let myself think about those last hours Stephanie and I spent with Noel in the hospital room, excruciating hours when all hope had been taken from us, I am grateful we somehow knew instinctively to inject humor as we talked our husband and father across to the other side. Stephanie's stories of her antics brought about some laughter, albeit forced, and I know, without question, Noel could hear and appreciate the levity.

I would never suggest that widows stop crying when periods of anguish strike; that's unrealistic, unacceptable, and probably impossible. Besides, a good cry is cathartic. Lord knows I cried a great deal more often than I laughed during those early months after my loss. Eventually it became clear, however, I had to start giving equal time to laughter because this held the power to cleanse my grief. Every time I was asked to go to someone's home for a glass of wine and some talk, I knew laughter would be an integral part of the gathering. Therefore, it was rare that I refused an invitation. Likewise I also made those events happen in my own home because the wine flows both ways. Even now when I become disheartened I try to remember what my husband loved most, and that always included humor. Perhaps one of the best ways I can be sure his memory lives on is my ability to laugh, even uproariously!

FIFTEEN

don't ignore the signs around you

Make yourself familiar with the angels, and
behold them frequently in spirit,
for without being seen, they are present with you.
-St. Francis de Sales

One December morning, when I was well into my third year of widowhood, my dear friend Marge and I were driving to Savannah to Christmas shop. We were talking about the latest book we had read, The Da Vinci Code when she asked, "What is the most significant spiritual discovery you made after Noel died?" My answer needed no forethought and was immediate. "The reality of his presence around me," I responded. My close friends excluded, most people will smile somewhat sadly at that statement and say, "Of course he is with you," and then quickly add, "Because he is always in your heart." This is true. The first couple of years after his passing there wasn't a day I awoke that he wasn't my first thought. However, it wasn't then, nor is it now, nearly as reassuring to acknowledge Noel's presence in my heart as it is to say with assurance, "He is with me because his spirit is around me, and he makes that obvious upon occasion by the signs that he sends!" Thus it is recognizing and accepting the signs the spirit of a loved one may be sending that is so important. While this may not always happen with the regularity we desire, every widow should work diligently to avoid throwing away the gift of communication because of skepticism!

For three decades I taught the literary concept 'willing suspension of disbelief' to high school sophomores, and joy of joys, they got it! They came to understand that in order to fully appreciate Shakespeare's A Midsummer Night's Dream, they had to set aside skepticism, if only temporarily, and buy into the notion that all things cannot be explained using the parameters of so-called reality. Even the existence of fairies, sprites, and yes, spirits, can be accepted for the duration of five acts, and inevitably the subject was treated with more serious consideration than I might have expected from a group of pseudo-sophisticated sixteen year olds. How ironic then, for all of the time I taught this delightful piece of literature, I viewed the premise simply as a vehicle by which I could get kids to enjoy a Shakespearean comedy rather than another level of reality deserving serious consideration for my own life.

Some people have an extremely refined capacity for recognizing the signs; I do not. I feel I have been very fortunate to be given experiences that have changed my life, but then I have had a great deal of guidance from somewhere. Nevertheless, I would like to believe that with some concerted effort, everyone can experience connection with a loved one who has transitioned. I don't pretend to know how to develop the capacity, nor would I want any woman to think if she doesn't receive communication, she isn't trying hard enough. All I am suggesting is every person should try to remain open to the possibility. Furthermore, given my feelings about letting go of mind-numbing sadness and opening one's self to humor and laughter, perhaps I subconsciously expanded myself and became able to detect what was already around me.

One bewildering aspect of my loss was foregoing the delight of being able to finish Noel's thoughts and his predisposition to do the same for me. We used to laugh at how I could distractedly mumble something that would never make sense to another person but was somehow crystal clear to him. So often he would know precisely what I intended to say. We called it the 'communications comfort zone'. Thus I am suggesting, perhaps, the ability to communicate is not lost with the passing of a person, and maybe the envelope has to be pushed a bit because the divide existing between here and there is one of unfamiliar territory. Moreover, it may not be a divide as we think of it. Of course the greatest dilemma that comes with this kind of thinking is when you ask yourself whether or not what you have experienced is real or your over-active imagination. Despite the number of connections I know Noel has made with me, there is still a small bit of skepticism that gnaws at me and demands every time I question whether or not I have willed this to happen. As you read the following stories, remember I questioned each and every one, not only when they happened, but also in the days that followed. Realize, too, they occurred not just early on when my emotions were raw and I was vulnerable, but much later when I was considerably beyond the period of mind paralysis. You may decide, as I have, there is very little wiggle room for skepticism.

I have spoken of the wind chimes, the Mother's Day card, and the appearance of the missing bank statement and checks. The first two incidents happened in May, just one month after Noel had passed away. It was that same month I decided I should try to regain some normalcy and a good way to start would be to get back with my ladies golf group. The first morning I determined I would play regardless of how tired or disinterested or depressed I might be, and so I set my alarm for 7:30 am...or so I thought. The buzzing noise awoke me at 7:30, but as I turned it off and lay there looking at the clock, I noticed the alarm was set for 8:30- I doubled checked to make sure I was seeing it correctly. The clock that was set for 8:30 had gone off at 7:30, the time I needed to get up. I am not a morning person, and there had been so many times when I would ignore the alarm and not get out of bed. That morning I smiled to myself and said, "OK, OK, I wasn't trying to get out of golfing today!"

Perhaps I should interject here that after I returned from that first visit to Lily Dale I found myself tentatively looking for signs that Noel was around, and, of course, those times when expectations are high are the times when absolutely nothing happens. What I discovered is these startling yet wonderful incidents come about when you least expect it.

I was never one to read the cartoons but always went straight to the editorials, the latest update on the world's happenings. My resident scientist, on the other hand, read the cartoons with gusto and appreciation, and they were the first section of the paper he grabbed. I used to kid him about the respective levels of intelligence, based upon our preference of newspaper sections. However, one Sunday morning in November, just before Thanksgiving, I was again sitting on the porch with my coffee and the paper. I started to toss aside the cartoons as usual, but something stopped me, and instead I began looking through them. Family Circus often shows those touching slices of life to which we all can relate, and on this morning the message was there for the taking. Seated around the Thanksgiving table was the entire family with the exception of the grandfather who had recently passed away. One of the young children asked whether or not Grandpa was enjoying the holiday in heaven. The reader had a view of the adjoining room where the spirit of the grandfather was sitting in the recliner, watching football on the television. This was a meaningful moment for me, one that spoke volumes, including the speculation Noel probably has a recliner in another dimension, and he watches every game his much-loved Pittsburgh Steelers play. For a while, I continued to access Family Circus in the hope another message for me might find its way there. It didn't.

The first winter after Noel passed away I knew the holidays were going to be difficult, and I had no notion how our family would get through them. However there were small children in the family for whom we had to prepare, and Noel would have been outraged by any diminishing of these normally joyful times. No one immersed himself in the holiday season more than my husband. Thus Jennifer and I decided we would spend Thanksgiving at her home and Christmas in Beaufort.

My mother had surgery planned for the week after Thanksgiving, and I made arrangements to be with her at her home when she returned from the hospital to recuperate. After spending three days there, I started back to Beaufort, having made it through my first major holiday without my husband. At the last minute I decided to stop in a nearby town and browse in a small art gallery. After an hour's stay it was time to get back on the road, and I headed out of town. I had not taken notice of the street names when I entered, and I found myself turned around, unsure of how to get back to the main road. I drove on several streets, finally stopping to take stock of where I was. I looked up at the street sign and to my amazement I found I was traveling on N. Lucas Street. While I was lucid enough to know that N designates north, that day, N. Lucas Street took on an entirely different meaning, and it guided me to the road that took me home.

A month later, my friend and I returned to the same little town forty miles away, and I found the area in question. I was worried I might have imagined the entire incident, and I wanted to make sure this wasn't the case. She took a picture of the sign, and for a long time it sat on the window sill above my sink as a reminder that not only was I not hallucinating but also that life can often be serendipitous.

For several years after my husband's passing, holidays without Noel were, without question, extremely painful. December was decidedly the worst; not only did we have to get through Christmas, the holiday he loved most, but also his birthday, the nineteenth of the month. The first Christmas we had somehow determined, without discussing it, we would take the stiff upper lip approach, and for a while it worked because we had the children to occupy us. My granddaughter Sydney was only seventeen months old, and on Christmas Eve I said I wanted to rock her before putting her to bed. What I really craved was some time alone to get rid of the tears I had been holding back. Thus I took her upstairs and settled into the rocking chair, and as I rocked my sweet granddaughter, the tears came in torrents. I looked down at her, knowing that I should stop weeping because I didn't want to frighten her. However, to my amazement, she was not looking at me at all but rather was staring at a spot close by. I followed her stare and saw nothing; her eyes, however, never shifted. As my crying began to subside and I gained control, I softly spoke her name, but again she did not react. Instead she continued to stare at the same spot for at least another minute, and during that time I was simply unable to distract her. I knew then that Noel was with us; he saw my pain, and Sydney was observing him through the innocent eyes of a small child, eyes capable of seeing so much more than adults comprehend with their learned sophistication.

Noel had always loved a live Christmas tree, and when we moved to our new home where there is a tree farm a half mile down the road, there was no question our holiday trees would be real and large, really large! He was like a kid in all his glory, and I have a picture of him in our small convertible, top down, bringing a huge tree to the back of the house the first Christmas we were in our home. After he passed away, I tried to keep up that short-lived tradition, but found it was unrealistic and so bought a ten-foot artificial tree, what I thought would be a compromise.

The day after Thanksgiving, our third without Noel, my son-in-law offered to assemble the Christmas tree, with my daughter and my granddaughters helping me to decorate. I put a sleeve of six Christmas CDs into the stereo, and we trimmed the tree for several hours, taking time out for dinner and finishing about nine o'clock in the evening. Everyone was tired, and by ten o'clock we were all in bed. I found I talked to Noel most often during the time between turning off the lights and falling asleep, and this night was no exception. I told him how much I wished he had been with us to see the two little girls' delight when we pulled out each ornament he and I had collected over our many years together. And I added that I wished I could know for certain he had observed this warm family tradition being carried forth.

The next morning I got up around eight thirty, and when I came out of my bedroom, Jennifer asked in a somewhat concerned voice whether or not I had gotten up during the night, and if I did, had I turned on the stereo. Of course my answer to both questions was, "no", and she responded that David had heard the music come on around three o'clock in the morning. Knowing Jennifer's discomfort with the direction this conversation was taking, I suggested perhaps there had been a power surge during the night and added I would check the phone and the microwave, two very sure indicators of an interruption of electricity. Neither showed a blinking light, and as I returned to the living room, the song playing on the sound system was The First Noel.

Admittedly the power for the stereo had been left on the night before. Equally important, however, is the fact that leaving the power on after a sleeve of CDs has played to conclusion happens frequently because I forget to turn off the system more often than not. Furthermore it can be days until I discover this omission. Never has the sound started up again unless I hit the play button. This was a situation where I was not anticipating anything, thereby making it a reality. Furthermore, the last people to conjure up this event are my daughter and son-in-law. Those who are skeptical can chalk it up to unexplained coincidence; I choose to believe Noel gave me a sign, answering my wish for confirmation of his presence at the tree trimming, and I could not have received a more beautiful gift.

On a later occasion I had another blip on the spiritual screen, and this time it wasn't courtesy of my husband. An indication that my receptivity to such messages had expanded beyond those of Noel came the day I returned from the funeral of a friend. Annie had suffered a debilitating stroke, leaving her comatose and clinging to life for several weeks. As she slowly emerged from this state, her quality of life was vastly diminished, one she would not have chosen. I often visited her in the nursing facility to which she had been moved, and her eyes told me of her pain, both physical and emotional.

My friend had been very supportive when I lost Noel, and she was fully attuned to all that was happening in my life after he passed away. We would often walk together in the evening, and she talked about her sister-in-law who is a medium, relating incidents that spoke to this woman's authenticity. Thus Annie and I were solidly connected by our belief in life after this one. The evening after her funeral, I was cleaning my bathroom and thinking about her. I spoke to her in my mind, saying, "Annie, I wish it could have been different for you at the end because you were a good person who deserved better." At that point, I had cleared everything from the sink area except a ceramic container in the shape of a girl who looks somewhat like the cartoon character, Cathy. After washing and drying it, I turned it over. The name Annie was engraved on the bottom, not Ann, but Annie. In the time that I have owned that piece of pottery, I never realized it was named, much less named Annie. Was it a coincidence? Perhaps, but that night I chose to believe otherwise, and I smiled to a place where I hoped my tousled-haired friend might be observing my discovery, hoping she knew that I knew.

Some will conclude that my imagination had overtaken my rational thinking on these occasions, making easily explained coincidences into more than they were. I don't accept this premise, and why should I? Skeptics will see me as anything but grounded, but my belief in all that happened provided me with an anchor that continues to make my life much more secure. I believe it is inherent upon all of us to work at making ourselves receptive to the messages that are around us. Don't ignore the signs. They may be frightening to some, and to others they may seem best ignored. For me, the times when I believe Noel sent his reassurance are priceless gifts that keep on giving, and I will never let my skepticism override what my heart tells me is real, even if I don't completely understand the message or its origin. As I stated before, if we knew all of the answers, there would be no room left for faith, and without it we would be lost.

SIXTEEN

on the wings of a butterfly

*Just when the caterpillar thought the world
was over, it became a butterfly.*
-anonymous

One of the more perceptible signs I believe Noel sent to me came about when I least expected it, as was often the case. Because there were many what-ifs that accompanied this incident, I have chosen to treat it separately. I have to think as you read what follows, you, too, will question just how much can be attributed to coincidence.

If there is a single book I recommend as a must-read for widows, it is *On Life after Death* by Elisabeth Kubler-Ross. I received a copy of this small but powerful work from one of Stephanie's friends whom I have known since she and my daughter were in grade school together. This young woman, who is as delightful an adult as she was a child, flew from Colorado to South Carolina to visit us shortly after Noel passed away. As we sat on the porch in the summer dusk, we reminisced about how he had helped the girls with their school science projects, and Merryl cried as she spoke emotionally of 'Science Man Lucas,' reminding me once again of just how many lives my husband had touched over the years. Later in the evening she talked at length of the power of Kubler-Ross' work, and she promised to send me a copy.

When the book arrived the following week, I sat down to read it right away, and I knew immediately it would play an important role in my search for answers to so many mystifying events that had happened since my husband's passing. Sadly, in the summer of 2004, I learned of the passing of Dr. Kubler-Ross, a bright intuitive whose writing so impacted my thinking during my time of grief and introspection. While she is well-known as the individual who identified the stages of grief, she also believed there are stages leading to the moment of death, and she used language taken from conversations with terminally ill children to explain her thesis. It was her analogy in comparing the death of the human body to that of a butterfly's emerging from the cocoon that grabbed my attention and wouldn't let go. In her book she asserts that as soon as the cocoon is in an irreparable condition, it releases the butterfly; in the case of the body, the soul is released. In the ensuing weeks, as I reread these passages, I became determined to find a photograph of a butterfly emerging from its cocoon and have it framed. I thought about resources such as *National Geographic* or perhaps a book on butterflies, but after a few weeks of searching, it appeared finding such a picture wasn't going to be as easy as I had anticipated. This is where the story takes on a serendipitous quality, and it was one of the many messages that assured me I was navigating the waters properly as I continued to seek answers to the questions that confound me.

It happened on a Friday morning, almost a year after I lost Noel. I had attended a meeting downtown and afterward decided to explore some of the new shops that seemed to have sprung up during the months I was trying to get my life back on track. I stopped at a small art gallery on Bay Street, and as I entered, I remembered my quest for the butterfly picture. The gallery owner was talking with another woman, so I waited for them to conclude their conversation. Finally the owner turned and asked if she could help me. When I told her what I was looking for, she shook her head, saying she had no idea where I might find such a photo. The second woman, who was still within earshot, spoke up and said, "Oddly enough, I was with someone last week whose husband has photographed exactly what you are describing." She went on to say this man had done a sequence of photos, and she would take my name and phone number and get in touch with the individual in question. Three days later I received a call from the photographer saying he would be glad to email all the pictures he had taken and create a copy of the one I preferred. I went to his home later the same week and was given the most exquisite image of a fully emerged Monarch butterfly with the cocoon still intact on the greenery. This framed picture sat for many years in my bedroom, a quiet reminder not only of my acceptance of the way Noel departed this world, but also of the far reaching implications of so-called coincidence. I see every aspect of this series of events as something much greater, perhaps helped along by my husband. Stephanie's friend *happened* to send the book by Kubler-Ross. I focused on the butterfly image in her book and *happened* upon the woman in the art gallery who *just happened* to have had the conversation with a friend regarding her husband's photo of the emerging butterfly. John Edward insists he does not believe in coincidence, and I contend this story is strong support for his assertion.

Perhaps I invest too much in the butterfly imagery, but this has come to hold a great deal of meaning for me. When I see one of these delicate creatures, regardless of where I am, I stop to take in the beauty and grace. It fills me with a sense of peace, so much so that my garden has acquired two butterfly bushes as well as an iron butterfly sculpture. At one time my checks supporting the Lupus Foundation were imprinted with muted butterflies, always a reminder of the image Kubler-Ross offered. This was one more small but powerful example that moved my healing forward.

SEVENTEEN

to sleep, perchance to dream

"Have you ever dreamt of someone who's gone,
Charley, but in the dream you have a new conversation?
The world you enter then is not so far
from the world I'm in now."
For One More Day
-Mitch Albom

When I began to write this memoir, I knew nothing about scientific theories of dreams and dreaming. In my research of Spiritualism, however, I encountered numerous sources addressing the nature of the dream world. My knowledge of the subject is still very limited, but I did discover one statistic that can be understood by everyone, something that should encourage all of us to pause and reconsider what information our dreams might impart. In *The Illustrated Dream Dictionary*, Russell Grant suggests on average we sleep a third of each day; by the time we are seventy-five, we have slept twenty-five years and have dreamed ten of those twenty-five. That's a lot of 'show time' by my calculation, and this statistic alone makes our dreams well worth the investigative effort.

The dreams I remember most vividly are an important part of my story, and I am convinced there is a reason why I experienced them. Periodically I replay the film when I am able, and I reflect upon the content that was so explicit in its detail. Each time I awakened from a dream and could recount minute points, even the smells I experienced, I knew these encounters differed from those vague nocturnal events that blur in the light of morning. Today, years after those dreams occurred, dreams I believe were contacts from my husband, I can describe them, and I return to my original conclusion that they played a pivotal role in heightening my sensitivity to what I used to ignore.

I cannot remember a time in my life when I didn't dream at night. As a child I don't recall waking because of nightmares, although I can remember the very generic dream in which someone or something was chasing me. Because my legs moved too slowly, I lost ground in my attempt to get away. However, the pursuer never took on a persona, and I am not sure why I was fleeing although Freud would surely have some thoughts about it.

Shortly after coming home from the hospital, having delivered our first daughter, I found myself sitting up in bed one night, searching through the blankets, "trying to find my baby." This, according to Noel, was what I said when he wakened me. I had this dream a couple more times, but since then I have read it is commonplace among new mothers, just another run-of-the-mill dream.

Once when Stephanie came to visit, I awoke one night to find her getting into my bed. As I got up to go to the bathroom, she indicated that she, too, was awake and had come to my bedroom because she had a frightening dream. Despite the fact that she was thirty-two, Mom's bed was every bit as inviting as it had been when she was a toddler, and I have to admit her seeking me out in the predawn hours was pure delight for my maternal ego, even if she had to leave a half hour later because I was snoring.

As I have said, there are times I can grasp fragments of my forays into the dream world when I first awake, and other times they are so vague as to be foggy notions of what *might* have happened. On those occasions when I experience a dream that is vivid and compellingly real, I pay very close attention and attempt to record every detail in the hopes I might derive some meaningful interpretation. What follows was one of those times.

The day before Noel passed away I experienced a dream I will always believe was a message from him telling me of his impending death. At four-thirty in the morning I received a phone call from the on-duty physician saying that Noel's heartbeat had become very irregular, and he wanted permission to use paddles in an attempt to correct the problem. Based upon my prior conversations with my husband, I had made it clear to the doctors that no extraordinary efforts were to be made to keep him alive on machines. This situation, however, was outside of those parameters, so I gave my permission and went across the street to hospital shortly afterward.

The doctors were still having some problems with him, but things settled into a lull of sorts. Around two o'clock that afternoon I told Stephanie I was going back to our room to try to nap. I removed my clothes and lay upon the bed, beyond exhaustion. At that point I settled into a kind of netherworld, somewhere between deep sleep and consciousness. I dreamed Noel was walking toward me. There was no setting around him; instead, the entire area was simply washed in a luminescent golden glow. I knew the moving figure was Noel, and I sat upright, believing at that moment he had passed away. I dressed quickly and ran across the street to the hospital to find that he was still alive, but now I am certain the dream was a message for me and that my husband entered my semi-conscious state to somehow alert me to what was about to happen. To this day the dream is starkly vivid, and I will always remember the feelings of despair it generated then and many times afterward.

Dreams that were very real and could be readily recalled became commonplace for me after I lost my husband. This had not been the case before. Two weeks after returning home from Baltimore, I awoke to Noel's voice in the early ether of dawn. It was utterly clear to me that he had come into the room and said, "Carol, are you up yet?" For a brief moment I was completely convinced that his passing had been a nightmare from which I was finally awaking. Of course, this wasn't the case, and my disappointment was so crushing that I wept in those dark, early morning shadows.

Perhaps the most powerful dream I experienced occurred a year after Noel's passing. He was a man who loved to hug; in fact, I have a friend who says Noel gave the best and most sincere hugs of any person she has ever known. I was experiencing a down week, one in which I cried for no particular reason other than the feelings of sadness that seemed to be smothering me. At one point I remember saying aloud, "Noel, more than anything I miss your coming from behind and hugging me." Two nights later I had a dream where I was in a very neat and clean barn. The interior walls were constructed of new wood, and the hay that was strewn about smelled fresh and pungent; the scents were very apparent and precise, and I took note of them as I walked around. To the right was a wide entrance to another room, and I recall thinking in the dream there had to be a large open window around the corner, because the light coming through the doorway was brilliant. Suddenly, Noel emerged from the doorway, and I gasped, "My God, Noel, you have come back." He said, "Carol, you didn't really think I would abandon you, did you?" With that he walked over and enclosed me in his arms, giving me the most wonderful hug. That dream remained with me for years, every detail clearly imprinted on my mind and providing comfort as I came to realize, indeed, he would not abandon me.

When I visited Lily Dale the second time, I asked Sherry Lee Caulkin, who places great emphasis on dreams and the messages they convey, what she thought the barn setting might mean. Her response was so simple I could hardly believe I had overlooked the obvious. She asked, "Did he ever work in or spend a great deal of time around a barn?" Noel grew up in the country and worked on a neighboring farm from the time he was twelve years old. It was only when he turned sixteen and began to drive that he took another job. The reality was he liked working out of doors and enjoyed returning to that kind of environment. As a young girl who was impressed by a muscular teenage boy, I loved the tan he sported every summer as a result of working in the fields without a shirt. Sherry Lee went on to say it appeared to her he was living on a farm on the other side and he chose to show this to me via the dream. Her response seemed so logical, and I was comforted by the thought that my husband now lived in a place so much to his liking.

It was a few months before the third anniversary of Noel's passing when I had a dream, a rather sad one, although I was not surprised by the message it contained. Much I have read about the soul's moving on, as well as the time it might linger around those loved ones here on earth, tends to support this very moving encounter. Noel and I were riding in our convertible. Everything was pleasurable about our trip together. He was driving, and at one point he turned to me and said, "You have to realize this is the last time we can be together like this." I was suddenly very sad and asked why. He responded simply, "You know why," and somehow I did.

It was the Greek playwright Aeschylus, speaking through the voice of Agamemnon, who said, "I know how men in exile feed on dreams of hope." Despite the seemingly final encounter with my husband on the vast plane somewhere between sleep and wakening, I continued to yearn that he would come back into my dreams, if only on the periphery. That wish was granted, and I did meet him again.

The date was April 9, 2004, exactly three years and one day after Noel had passed away. I was renovating a second home in North Carolina, a new project undertaken in hopes of refocusing my energies and my life. That evening I went out to the car to retrieve something forgotten, and as I started back to the house, I looked up into the clear night sky. Every star was precisely chiseled, and I stopped for a moment to enjoy the sheer wonder of it all. I hadn't let the previous day make me sad, because Stephanie had emphasized upon every anniversary since her Dad's passing there should be no forced mourning. "We don't miss him any more on April 8th than we do the rest of the year," she said. But as I looked at the heavens, I couldn't get past the need to talk to Noel, telling him again how much I missed him and how a shooting star right then might be a nice touch- a tall order, and no small presumption on my part.

Of course there was no shooting star, nor was there any other sign to indicate that he had heard me. The next night, however, I had a dream that retained its clarity when I awoke. Again, there was no discernible setting. Very simply, Noel and I were standing somewhere, and I turned to him and said, "Noel, do you still love me?" No prior circumstance in the dream called for this question, and he stood there and looked at me, never taking his eyes from mine. What he did then was enough for me in the dream and is sufficient answer for me now. Noel took my face in his two hands and kissed me in the same sweet way he always had. There was no need for words. My husband's love for me continues today as does mine for him, and if I patiently go about all I must accomplish in this life, I believe I will be rewarded with a continuation of his love in the next life.

Stephanie and I talk frequently about the dreams that include her father, for she has experienced many of these as well. She expresses her delight over the communication in this way: "He simply drops in unannounced sometimes. When that happens I feel as though I have been given a gift. I know while I am dreaming he isn't supposed to be here any longer, but it's great that he is, isn't it?" We both welcome these occasional appearances, finding them to be remarkably comforting.

In the years following my husband's passing, the dream world became a place I consciously sought out before dropping off to sleep. I would talk to Noel in my mind and ask him to visit me in my dreams if it were possible. In the long run, it may have been my intense need to be with him, if only occasionally, thus creating this venue in my subconscious through wishful thinking. I will argue if this were the case, I fortunately had found a way to ease my mind and mend my heart. I began to look forward to going to bed at night because there was always the outside chance I could go to the place where nothing is impossible and communication with the man I still loved would occur, if only briefly.

Perhaps I was a wistful Shirley Maclaine wannabe; certainly this celebrity has written in- depth accounts of her night trips to astral planes beyond this world. Or, perhaps, with Noel's help, I had stumbled upon some connection to the other side. What I do know is this: anytime I dreamed of Noel and could recall that dream in vivid detail, I felt as though an undefined part of me had expanded, and I was given another perspective, something that would help me understand the new direction my life was taking.

Speculation about the origin of dreams and how to interpret them has a very long history, some of it compelling and some a bit melodramatic. Prophetic dreams have been the subject matter for a great deal of history and literature. Yet, I believe that today, in the twenty first century, we have only scratched the surface of what comprises the dream world. Furthermore, I am certain there will come a time when dreams will be widely recognized as a tool enabling us to interpret aspects of our lives that may well be part of another dimension. Until then, I choose not to deny my dreams but rather explore them.

Gradually, I have come to accept Noel's spirit isn't around as consistently as it was right after his passing. I hope my need to have access to him, if only in my dreams, has diminished to the point that he can move on. In this respect I may have lost him again, but I prefer to think of it as one more way I have helped him move forward in *his* journey, and it gives me a great deal of satisfaction and peace of mind. And maybe, just maybe, he will find time in the other dimension to take an occasional trip back. If so, I want the door to be wide open for him when he does.

EIGHTEEN

a little background music, please

And I believe that angels breathe, and that
love does live on and never leaves.
-To Where You Are
music by Richard Marx
lyrics by Linda Thompson
performed by Josh Groban

Music speaks to me in ways nothing else can; this has always been the case. When I was seven years old, I was chosen to sing "O, Holy Night" in the church Christmas Pageant, and I had to concentrate very hard not to cry during the performance. It wasn't because I suffered from stage fright but because the organ music was so beautiful and the words so exquisite. As I sang, "Fall on your knees, O, hear the angel voices," I could have done just that, even as a child. Today, this piece of music continues to affect me in the same way. Despite my failure to accept organized religion, even as a younger person, I appreciated then and still appreciate many pieces of religious music that touch the core of my being.

Whether it is vocal or instrumental, music has the potential to take me to imaginary places; often the words or the melody seem to be communicating to me alone. I can travel for miles in my car, surrounded by wonderful music, and discover I cannot remember the road I have traveled because other sights produced by that music have overtaken my conscious thoughts. Fortunately, this delight hasn't caused any accidents thus far.

The magic of music will often lead me to dance or sing or weep, any or all of which can happen spontaneously. This was the case long before I lost Noel, and it seemed to happen more frequently after he passed away. It was no surprise, then, that one of the more clarifying moments of my life came about as I listened to a beautiful and haunting song that put so much of my pain into perspective.

The Ally McBeal Show was a popular television program around the time I lost my husband, and although it has since disappeared from the small screen, the night Josh Groban appeared on the show will be forever etched in my mind. I was halfheartedly watching the program, my attention span having dwindled to almost nothing. The story line was a sentimental one, but by then everything I saw or heard was saturated with emotion; this was early in my grieving when a commercial featuring a child and a puppy would produce a cascade of tears. When the talented young man sang "To Where You Are," it was as though the heavens had opened and a choir of angels was singing just for me. I know I sat in Noel's chair, wracking sobs overtaking me until there were no more tears to be shed. The magnificence of Josh Groban's voice had consumed me, and for several moments I was unable to think or even move.

In ordinary times I would have gone out the next day and purchased Groban's CD. These, however, were not ordinary times. I barely had enough energy to move from the chair to my bed, let alone to think ahead. It was not until almost a year later, when I caught the end of an Oprah Winfrey show focusing on incredibly talented young people, that I saw Josh Groban for the second time. Again, he sang the same song whose lyrics were so intensely meaningful to me, and again I cried. Fortunately, by this time I had the presence of mind to jot down the necessary information, and the next day his CD was mine.

This musical masterpiece played an enormous role in my healing. A bit of research on the Internet revealed that Groban had dedicated the song to his late grandmother with whom he had a close relationship. Every time I listened to this this song, I was impressed by the flawless beauty of the music, but it was the intensity of the words that impacted me then as well as now. Those lyrics hold a promise we all long to hear and understand, and the reassurance we crave is as close as the push of the play button on a sound system.

"To Where You Are" became *my* song, the hook upon which I hung every thought and question regarding Noel's passage to the other side. I would inhale the words and my tears were endless; yet, oddly enough, they were tears of comfort. This went on for several months, and while eventually I lost what was most assuredly an obsession with the song, it continued to have special meaning for me. Even today, years later, I do not listen to this musical message without being reminded of its significance and how it helped to bring me out of the shadows of grief to a place where I began to function much better.

On the night of my sixtieth birthday, one year after Noel's passing, three friends took me to dinner. The plan was to meet at a favorite local seafood house that does not take reservations. One goes there with the hope of not having to linger more than forty-five minutes before being seated. When we arrived, we were told the wait would be an hour and a half. Dismayed by this news, and anxious to sit with a martini and talk, we decided to go to another restaurant twenty minutes away. There we were seated right away, and four chatty females immediately began to indulge in what comes naturally-animated talk and laughter. Eventually we quieted down long enough to choose from the menu. Playing in the background was my song, "To Where You Are."

Skeptics will say, "Not even close; coincidence at best!" Consider, however, that we could have been seated promptly at the first restaurant, but we weren't; or that we loved the first restaurant enough to wait for a table, which we didn't. Consider, too, that in the second restaurant we had talked our way through much of the early evening, hardly able to hear anything but our own voices, much less any music until, in that one brief, quiet moment "To Where You Are" became audible. I believe I was meant to hear my song on the occasion of my birthday, a gift from the man who had made all my birthdays special from the time I was sixteen years old.

Two weeks later I was on my way to the doctor. I was having problems with my back, and it was difficult for me to stay seated for long. As I drove, I talked to Noel in my mind, telling him how much I missed not having him around, specifically alluding to occasions such as these when he always insisted on taking me to a medical appointment. He knew I am a born coward when it comes to seeing a doctor, so he always made himself available. There I was, lying on the table, waiting for my physician to come in, and when I let my mind tune in to the music playing throughout the suite of rooms, the first song I heard was… well, you know. Just another nudge to tell me that if I thought the incident two weeks before was a fluke, I should be reassured that it wasn't.

And now, all you skeptics, listen up! Four years later, when the popularity of "To Where You Are" had diminished (not for me…never for me), I had an encounter with *my song* that was all the more telling, not only because of the time lapse but also because of my much-improved state of mind. In April of 2006, two of the three friends who had treated me to dinner on my sixtieth birthday did so again. This time Marge, Marilyn and I went to a newly opened restaurant, and as we stood in the foyer waiting to be seated, Marge turned to me and said, "There's your guy." I glanced around, looking for someone I might recognize when she said, "Listen." There it was again, Josh Groban singing "To Where You Are." Both of these women knew the story of *my song*, and when we all stopped to listen, we became very quiet. In *The Soul's Religion*, Thomas Moore includes a chapter he calls "Taking Angels Seriously." In it he asserts angels speak to us, offering messages that are crucial to our well-being. In one passage, one that makes so much sense to me, he addresses the musicality of these ethereal beings. He writes:

> "Angels are not only guardians and messengers, but also musicians. Paintings of angels show them playing every instrument imaginable and singing. I

remember over a decade ago realizing one day that the glorious paintings of angel musicians teach that all music with the power to move us is the playing of angels."(p. 148)

Noel and I both sang in the same high school and college choirs. We loved all genre of music, and there was always a wide range of tapes and, later, CDs in our home. The first luxury we allowed ourselves, right after we got married, was a good stereo system, and after our girls arrived, we often picked them up in our arms and dance around the room. Why then wouldn't my husband choose music as a way to connect with me?

In April of 2007, my older daughter, Jennifer, informed me that my birthday gift from her and her family was a ticket to see Josh Groban live in concert. It goes without saying that I was ecstatic! His appearance in Greenville, South Carolina was the first of the year in this country after his tour of Europe. The young man was even more magical on stage than he was on my sound system at home, despite the fact that, by way of apology, he told the audience he had contracted an upper respiratory infection on the flight back to the states. I sat mesmerized as I watched, in person, the individual whose pure and crystalline voice had helped draw me out of periods of sadness, those times that threatened to deplete any hope I might have had to regain firm footing in my world of widowhood. I was so grateful to have been given this opportunity, although I was a bit disappointed when the end of the show arrived, and he had not sung *my* song. Perhaps it was just as well he didn't sing "To Where You Are", because after such a delightful evening, I would have hated to embarrass my daughter by weeping as I still do on occasion when Josh Groban takes me to a place where I can almost feel Noel waiting for me.

NINETEEN

learning to live alone

Inside myself is a place where I live all alone,
and that's where I renew my springs that never dry up.
-Pearl Buck, American writer and humanitarian

In *The Wizard of Oz* Dorothy passionately proclaims, "There's no place like home!" While this declaration may be true for many people, for the newly widowed woman home is often a locale of contradiction and disquiet. When we finally gain the confidence and the will to venture beyond our four walls, we do so with some caution. When that time came for me, I found myself going out during the day and engaging in activities that took on a frenzied approach, rendering me the proverbial moving target; I suspect I came to rely upon the supposed inability to hit one of those. By the end of the day, I was positively depleted. However, the reality, is this: we still return to an empty house that holds so many memories as well as material reminders of what was, and sadly, what no longer is. The clicking of our red sequined shoes cannot change that fact.

Before Noel's passing, I had never lived alone. I was with my family until the time I left for college, then it was four years of dorm life where residing by yourself was viewed as a luxury but never an option. I married one semester prior to graduation and joined my husband to begin thirty-nine years of living together. I recall the times when Noel went on overnight fishing trips, and I was afraid to stay by myself. Later, even having the girls with me was not the same as his being in the house, so you can imagine the loneliness I faced when I returned to South Carolina.

Fortunately my daughter Stephanie decided to stay with me for six months before she took a permanent job in Atlanta. She worked close by on Fripp Island, and we spent countless nights talking into the early morning hours, working through the profound void confronting both of us. I will always be grateful for that period of time when my daughter put her life on hold for me. While I know it was advantageous for both of us to begin our healing together, I was so much better equipped to take on solitary living as a result of her presence during the time when my heartache was an open wound.

I don't want to give the impression that Jennifer and her husband were not a source of comfort because nothing could be farther from the truth. However, they lived two hundred miles away, and they had a family of their own. We kept in touch through visits and several phone calls during a week's time, and I have no doubt about their concern for me at a time when they, too, were grieving.

I am sure it is commonplace that many couples spend a great deal of time in the quiet company of one another, and I thoroughly enjoyed these periods 'solitary companionship.' Noel was a morning person, ready to do business when he got out of bed and his feet hit the floor. I, on the other hand, hated getting up early and saw any opportunity to sleep in as a real gift. Even so we were able to enjoy companionable time together over coffee and the newspaper on the weekends. He may have been up and active for three hours before I emerged from the bedroom, but he always sat down for another cup of coffee with me. Thus it was that my morning routine was terribly disconcerting for a long time.

One evening, after Stephanie had taken a job in Atlanta, she called to talk, and she said, "I purposely called now because I want to know if you are eating dinner standing over the sink?" I laughed and said I was in the process of preparing my meal, and as usual my dinner companion that evening would be Peter Jennings. It is sad irony that I lost my secondary dinner company to cancer as well. Meals were lonely, but I refused to let myself get into the habit of grabbing a quick bite while not sitting down, or worse yet, not eating at all. I found, however, the solitude of eating dinner alone at a table was too disconcerting. What I saw on television may not have been the best for my digestion, but it surpassed looking at the empty spot where another place setting had been.

I discovered driving alone on longer trips was intimidating because I had always been the navigator in the passenger seat. So when I embarked on my first six hour trip to a place I had never been, apprehension overtook me. How was I going to drive *and* navigate? I remember saying to Noel, wherever he might have been, "You have to help me with this, sweetheart, because if I don't make it work now, chances are I won't try it again." People speak of divine inspiration, and I have no problem believing it happens. Additionally, I defer once more to accepting everyone has a guardian angel. Whether inspired or angel driven, I decided before leaving I would make things as easy as possible for those unseen forces as well as for myself. This was before the advent of the now-commonplace GPS; back then for me those letters represented the opening of my prayer when I got into the car, "God, please save." The first thing I did was type the directions in large bold letters, print them, and keep them on the seat beside me. I did have a cell phone which gave me some sense of security. Then I put together a small basket of necessities, including finger foods. Finally, I included a couple of audio books. I discovered after the first trip this was a great way to travel. Much as I love music, a voice in the car provides a kind of companionship that music often does not. Certainly I miss the wonderful hours Noel and I spent talking to one another on a trip, and traveling alone isn't especially fun. However, I wasn't about to let myself become bound to a thirty-mile perimeter around my home, not if I could help it. I had discovered all too painfully how short life can be, and there is a lot out there to see.

The acceptance of being single after having been married for so long was a complex challenge for me. However, being alone and being lonely are two different issues. I was fortunate to have the support of my friends, many of whom are married, and I learned something I think many widows overlook. It takes a while to feel like doing anything social, and often we wait for an invitation. I caught on pretty quickly that if you make it clear you are comfortable being the only single person at a gathering- forget about whether or not you really are- real friends will take their cue. I would like to think when we were all together, there was no sense of the maudlin hanging overhead. I mentioned Noel's name quite frequently when I was with my friends, suggesting how he might have reacted to something that was said or done. In this way I made it clear that talk of him was not off limits, and I wouldn't break into tears should they refer to him.

One time I read a newspaper article about how women learn to cope with their loss, and I was taken by what one widow had to say. She offered, "It is a new normal. He's not here, but I feel like myself again." *A new normal.* A change certainly, but thank God, normalcy of some kind. I learned I didn't have to be lonely all the time if I worked at it, something well worth the effort. I found volunteering was therapeutic; it took my mind from my problems temporarily, and I was able to accept there were those with issues every bit as gut-wrenching as mine. I joined a local chorale and discovered this was a wonderful distraction. And after a few years, I was fortunate enough to become part of a writers' group that encouraged me to continue with the project you presently hold in your hands. Pouring out my thoughts, many times after midnight and into the morning hours, was what I needed most. By imposing some structure on my circumstances, I was able to slowly regain control of my life.

I would advise any widow to keep a journal when she gets to the point she can carve out the time and the energy to write. While you don't have to publish a book, note-taking will permit you to look back, and you will be surprised at the progress you made.

PART THREE

I can't change the direction of the wind,
but I can adjust my sails to always reach my destination.
-Jimmy Dean

TWENTY

lily dale, take two

The trouble is, if you don't risk anything, you risk even more.
-Erica Jong

Two summers after Noel passed away, I decided to travel outside the country. One of my trips took me on a cruise to Nova Scotia. Often I felt Noel with me as I sat alone on the deck and watched the sun sink below the watery horizon. Again, when I climbed the cliffs above the water in Acadia National Park, I simply knew he was feeling my wonderment as I soaked in the surroundings and wistfully thought about how much he would have enjoyed this trip.

Later that summer I traveled to Provence, and the French countryside spoke emotional volumes to me. One day I visited a large cathedral in the city of Avignon, and I lighted a candle for Noel. Despite my aversion to organized religion, I felt compelled to acknowledge my husband in this holy place…I know, a little hypocrisy in play. The candle I used had a slightly different appearance from the others already there, and the only space I could find to place it was close to the bottom of a multilevel, spiral candle holder. I toured the rest of the massive stone structure, and when I was leaving, I returned to the room of candles. A nun was rearranging many of them, and I noticed the one I had placed near the bottom tier had been moved to a much higher position. I smiled, hoping it was a sign that perhaps I had nudged my husband along his path just a bit. By then, I was beginning to appreciate the importance of my experiences, some impressive, others more subtle. Yes, I was still dealing with my loss, and decidedly I was traveling a road that often frustrated and frightened me. Yet this journey was taking me to some beautiful and serene places that offered insights, many of which seemed to help me move along. It became my task to not only notice them, but also to use them, perhaps to weave a canopy beneath which I might retreat when the darker clouds moved in, as they invariably did.

Finally it came time for me to return to Lily Dale, the small town where my life had taken a radical turn. Eventually I would come to view my visits here as a layering process. It was two years later, to the day, when I drove to Lily Dale for the second time. I was traveling alone this time because MD had decided one visit was sufficient for her. After all she had her own channel tuned in, so why waste time clicking the remote, only to find more of the same? The day was overcast and dreary, with intermittent rain, not at all like the sun-drenched day she and I had enjoyed the first time. Lack of familiarity was no longer an issue, but even so I had no idea of what to expect. Certainly my mental state was light years better than when I had first visited. Furthermore, I was going to see Christine Wicker who had come back to Lily Dale for a book signing of her recently published book on the community of mediums. Nevertheless, it was with the same combination of euphoria and hesitancy that I entered the gate and drove to the Takei home.

As I settled in, I felt a bit less like the outsider I had been before. After all, my story had been told in Christine's book, and at a party held the next evening for her, it was fascinating to speak with some of the Lily Dale residents and answer their questions. Mine could hardly be construed as celebrity status; nevertheless, the people there were interested in my experience, and I knew they were folks who didn't find what I had to say strange or even unusual.

Mentally, I tried to avoid any replication of my first visit. In the intervening two years, I had been given enough reinforcement outside the realm of Lily Dale to be fairly certain of the whereabouts of Noel's spirit. If Sherry Lee Caulkin were correct in her interpretation of my dream two years ago, the one where I met Noel in the new barn with all the fresh hay, then I believed he was still residing there, visiting me when the need seemingly increased. Thus I had no desire for my second visit to the Dale to mirror the first, and what I hoped for was something fresh. That said, when Shelley Takei told me I had my choice of eight bedrooms, I chose to stay in the same room where I had slept the first time, simply because it seemed the thing to do. No intentions of trying to replicate?

I spent the first two days in the town leisurely wandering about, trying to assess my feelings. I acknowledged to myself I was a very different person now. Of course I was still feeling the loss of Noel; yet I had come to a state of ease no longer disrupted by the many meltdowns that were prevalent two years before. Finally, after walking up and down Lily Dale's streets, absorbing the ambiance much like a squirrel gathering nuts to sustain herself for the upcoming winter, I went to my scheduled reading with Martie Hughes who by now had become a registered medium in the town. No back porch chance happening this time, although you will never convince me the first encounter was one of chance.

By the time I came face to face with Martie for the second time, I had toyed with the idea of writing a book on widowhood, a catharsis for myself as well as possible support for countless women who fluctuate between the raw pain and numbing despair the loss of a soul mate produces. My approach would be different from that of the usual self-help book because my solace was derived, in large part, from spiritual contact with my husband. Standing back and looking at authoring a book written in this light, I had concerns that made me vacillate between sheer determination and troubling uncertainty. Perhaps the unspeakable loss of a man who has meant everything to a woman should remain just that, unspoken. Would I have the ability or the energy to tap into the wellspring of my own anguish and commit to paper details so poignant and private to me? Could I take the chance of putting my pain out there or subjecting myself to the disappointment of hearing publishers say that my story isn't particularly good reading? These were questions I considered from the beginning when writing a book seemed, if nothing more, a way to attain some relief for my hurt. Often I would dismiss the idea of publishing and tell myself those hours spent at the computer-often into the early hours of morning-were cheaper than time spent on a psychiatrist's couch at two hundred dollars an hour! I suppose I didn't want this to be one more disappointment or setback for my fragile state of mind.

When I first arrived at Martie's house, she said that Noel had "appeared" earlier but that she told him he was too early, urging him to come back. That's my guy! Always insistent on being at any appointment ahead of time. If Christine Wicker had been present she might have said, "Eye-rolling quotient" meaning in this case, "You have to be kidding that Martie would direct Noel's spirit to come back later." But then, he was a pretty accommodating guy when he was alive, and I can't think he would devolve into rudeness after crossing over.

So there I was at last, sitting across from the medium who had shaken my world two short years before, receiving messages once again from Noel. "He wants to know when you are going to write your book," she said with the trace of a smile playing across her lips and a twinkle in those incredibly blue eyes. Her voice, however, held its usual "I-brook-no-nonsense" edge. My response was purposely flippant when I countered, "Well, since he sees *everything*, he already knows I have notes in my computer." She allowed herself a full-blown laugh and retorted, "And he says all three of us know that notes in a computer do not make a book."

"He says you should begin with the dedication, and then move to the acknowledgments. He thinks that by doing this you will pay tribute to all of those people who have been important to you on this journey. Furthermore, he stresses you should devote a chapter to each person, even if they turn out to be short chapters." This was a rather amusing directive from a chemistry teacher who didn't particularly like to write and had relied upon me to generate any communication that went public under his name. But later, as I thought about it, his message made a great deal of sense. There were so many people who had nurtured me and had undertaken the task of mending me, getting me to where I am today. I might add that although I have not structured my book in this exact manner, I have paid close attention to integrating those who were by my side from the moment my husband was hospitalized, through those horrific days when he lay comatose, and the years well beyond as I was making headway toward attaining my new normal. My story would be nothing without them.

"He also says he will be with you and help you every step of the way," she added. Of course he would. The man had spent his entire life helping me through innumerable projects, not only during our professional lives teaching together in the same high school, but also on a personal level. I remember well the time we decided to wallpaper the bathroom right after we moved into our house in Pittsburgh. It was an older home, and the walls were anything but plumb. When we got to the corner behind the toilet, I was standing on the seat trying to manipulate the paper so it would be straight. Several times we thought we had it, but invariably the outside edge was crooked. After many attempts, my sweet and ordinarily patient husband tore the sheet from the wall, wrapped it around me as I stood on the toilet seat, and said, "Wallpaper your own damned bathroom!" Then he stormed out the door and down the steps. There I was, encased in blue and white paper, looking like a mummy whose wrappings were slipping. At first I was furious, but then I started to giggle and ultimately was consumed by gales of laughter. Noel came back up the steps, peeked into the bathroom, looking a little sheepish I might add, and mumbled something like, "Lookin' good, my dear." We did finish the job together, but decided that if anything might take a marriage to the brink of dissolution, it could be the job of wallpapering together. Despite the bathroom debacle, we continued to attack other jobs as a twosome, and we worked very well as a team. Even after we moved into our new home in Beaufort, when Noel began laying a brick sidewalk, I carried bricks in a wheel barrow to him, adding brick tender to my resume.

If Noel's game plan for my book had constituted Martie's entire reading, I would have shrugged it off and speculated that she saw this as a way to push me toward doing what I had mused about aloud in an earlier conversation. I commented wryly that if I ever wrote a book, it would have to contain a chapter entitled "Going to Bed with John Edward." I was referring to the well-known medium whose television program, *Crossing Over,* had become a large force in my life. For several months after Noel had passed away, I watched this program every night when I crawled into my empty bed at eleven o'clock. It gave me comfort I came to depend upon as I tried to work through the sadness that had become my life. I had spoken of this to a group of people in a social setting that included Martie, so I didn't find her reference to book writing a startling revelation.

However, Noel's message that addressed the penning of my story was only part of my hour-long session during which any shred of skepticism I may have tried to retain over the past two years was torn away and discarded. As I sat across from the woman who had entered my life two years ago on the wings of a golf angel, my husband evidently felt compelled to give me one more bit of proof that he was around and aware.

Martie continued her reading by announcing Noel was there and he was holding a small black notebook in his hands. She said she could not tell what was in the notebook but it was somewhat smaller than a three ring binder. Then she paused and said, "Oh, for heaven's sake! It's a photo album, and it contains all black and white photos. They are very dated, the type that have the serrated edges, and some of them are of Noel as a young kid." *That* got my attention!

Earlier in the week, when I had been staying with MD, she and I spent time in the Summerville Library looking through folders and binders that contained pictures dating back to the time when my grandfather was a young man. The library had become a repository for old photos, pictures that would eventually be organized and serve as a pictorial history of the town. My roots are in Summerville, Pennsylvania, and I was delighted to find several old class pictures, many of which were composites of the various classes that had passed through the school system. When I came upon pictures of Noel's class from elementary school, I put them into a tote bag I was carrying, intending to duplicate them and return the originals. The same was true of pictures of my grandfather, my cousin, and my uncle. All the photos in question were black and white, and some had serrated edges.

This information was never conveyed to anyone in Lily Dale. My photographic discoveries from a few days before had nothing to do with my Lily Dale activities. Furthermore, my friend hadn't accompanied me, so this could not be attributed to her having made a revealing comment. As the reading proceeded, Martie went on to say an older man, who was smoking a pipe, was present. At first I thought it might have been my dad until she said the man was wearing an apron that seemed to be smeared and dirty. My grandfather was a butcher by trade, and I often visited him in the store when I was small. A stained apron was part of his apparel for as long as I can remember. He also smoked a pipe. Martie indicated this man spoke of happy times when we were all together, and she asked whether or not he had lived with us. Actually, we lived with my grandparents for two years, and I forged a very strong relationship with my grandpa. He loved me dearly, to the point that often he would not permit my parents to discipline me. During my time in the library when I discovered the pictures of him, I talked to him quietly in my mind. Perhaps I had unknowingly summoned him as I browsed through the photos of a man who meant a great deal to me when I was growing up. For me this connection was as meaningful as that with Noel, and my grandfather would have understood this.

The reading continued with the comment that Noel wanted me to know he was aware one of our mutual friends was experiencing a couple of problems, and he knew I would help her by staying connected with her as long as she needed me. It is unnecessary to add specifics to this part of the reading or to identify the person in question. However, he gave Martie the name, and the use of the word "couple" was significant in that this person was, indeed, dealing with two separate dilemmas, something the medium could not have known.

After returning from my first visit to Lily Dale, I told a friend about the readings I had received. She didn't approve of my venture into the realm of the spiritual and told me because I was vulnerable, I would accept anything. As hurtful as the comment was at the time, memory of it served me well after Martie's reading this time, because I was not bringing to the table a mind totally diminished by grief. I was no longer intensely vulnerable. With certainty, I knew those readings were not an aberration and knew also I would return to Lily Dale again, as often as I felt it was necessary. Being there did nothing to hurt or delude me, but rather gave me courage that carried me through the toughest time of my life. Two years later, further validation was set before me, and it was mine for the taking.

TWENTY-ONE

it's not all about me

A great soul serves everyone all the time.
A great soul never dies.
It brings us together again and again.
-Maya Angelou

If I had been the only person receiving messages from my husband, I might have been less inclined to accept, without any questioning, their validity. I want to make it clear that I tried very hard to keep my skepticism firmly in place throughout all that had happened; to do otherwise may have invited responses ranging from pity to disgust. However, a large part of the reason I have come to believe Noel's spirit remained around us for so long came from stories other people told me. The diversity of the people involved and the circumstances under which these connections took place beg consideration.

You must understand that my husband was the person everyone loved, really loved. He simply had no enemies.

When my daughters talk about their father, they insist he never gossiped, and often say they cannot recall his speaking negatively about anyone. Does this mean that Noel was a pushover who never had an opinion? Not a chance! The man was quite capable of cursing with the best of them, and he could be incredibly obstinate at times, refusing to budge from a stance that he would later admit he knew was wrong. The wallpaper escapade certainly underscores that. But there was no meanness about him, and it was his kind and gentle nature that drew people to him.

One early instance of Noel's communication with someone other than me occurred with a friend who was very close to both of us. We saw Sherrill through a divorce, and later, when she remarried, her second husband and Noel became the best of friends. Our families frequently vacationed together, and for a while she and I delighted in the possibility that her son and our daughter would become serious about one another. They were the couple with whom we were closest, and I know they felt the loss of my husband profoundly. When I spoke to her after returning from Baltimore, this is the story she told me.

Sherrill knew Noel was in the hospital and not doing well. However, not having heard anything to the contrary, she continued to hold out hope. The night Noel passed away, she had a dream that she maintains was more vivid than any she can remember having had. Noel came to her, and she told him he looked wonderful, very healthy. Amazed by this, she said, "Noel, I thought you were really sick and not doing well, but you look great." Noel replied, "I was very sick, but I am much better now." She assumed when she awoke he had surely come out of his comatose state and must be doing better. When a mutual friend called later in the day to say he had passed away, she believed then her dream had been a visitation from Noel, and that he was no longer dealing with his illness after having crossed over. It was three days before she could call to talk, and when she did call, the conversation was thick with emotion. I might add my friend and I, until that time, had never engaged in any discussions regarding communication from the deceased.

After visiting Lily Dale for the second time, I came back to Pittsburgh for my return flight to South Carolina. Before I left town I decided to visit the school where Noel and I had taught together most of our careers. It was summer, and I knew I was taking a chance on seeing the staff that might be there and missing those who would be on vacation. However, I hoped to see some of the secretaries who were still good friends. The school had been remodeled after I retired, and I was unfamiliar with the new administrative wing where these women now worked. At the time I hoped I wouldn't have difficulty finding their new offices.

I entered a hall that was dimly lighted and stopped to get my sense of direction when a restroom door opened and out walked my friend, Ann. She stepped back and gasped audibly when she saw me. Then she realized who it was, and we had a great reunion. Later we went to her office, and, with the door closed, Ann said to me, "I am sure you observed my reaction when I came out and saw you, but I don't think you know *why* I reacted in such an extreme way." I laughed and said I thought she was just surprised to see me since she didn't know I was coming. "Yes, I was surprised, but that isn't what brought about my response," she stated quietly. "When I came out into the hall, there was such a bright light behind and surrounding you that I really couldn't see who you were." She went on to say she had to look closely to identify me, but it was the light that astounded her. Ann was Irish and very spiritual, and she said this had happened to her "only a handful of times." She remained certain, even years later, that the light was Noel's spirit. Ann passed away not long ago, and I like to think she and my husband have met over there and compared notes.

In May of 2004, there were two instances when Noel made his presence known to people in Pittsburgh, both teachers with whom we had taught. The first was with my friend Linda, an individual whose name will appear later as part of my third reading in Lily Dale. Linda taught in the same school district as we did, she in the middle school. Over the years this association became a solid friendship that continued even after we moved south. One day I received an e-mail from her stating she had been diagnosed with multiple myeloma. She had debated whether or not to tell me, knowing how difficult Noel's passing had been for me. Nevertheless, when I learned of her health problems, I called immediately, and we spoke at length. Two months later I received the following communication:

"Dear Carol, I want to tell you about a different experience that I had shortly after you called me. If this were years ago and we were at the pool, you would laugh and think I was nuts. I went to see a psychic at a place called Indian Summer. I went because I have for many years wanted to do this and figured I could never afford to "waste" the money. I guess after a certain age, when family and friends have passed, there are more opportunities for those who are gone to make contact. The psychic said that there were two teachers who had died of cancer there with us. I said the only person I had known from school was Noel, and I only knew him slightly but that you and I were close friends. He said that Noel had recently been around me, and that the disease that they thought I had I do not have. I guess he was watching over Mount Lebanon Internal Medicine. He said that you and Noel were very close, like one, but that you were opposites. I thought about Noel teaching Science and you English, and I do think that is very opposite. I could not think of another person that I knew that died of cancer; then I remembered my college roommate. We never taught together as she moved to California. She died in her 30's. He said she taught "special" kids- she was a special ed teacher. So many people came through. I do believe there is life beyond what we live here on earth. Hope this is comforting and not upsetting. With love, Linda."

What Linda failed to consider is Noel and I had markedly different personalities as well; some might say polar opposites. Her medium had been right on target with his assessment of us as a couple.

And yes, Noel did manage to connect with two males, in case you are wondering about his tendency to visit only our female friends. As I think about it, however, I am left with this conjecture: the fact that Noel did connect with MD, Sherrill and Linda tells me perhaps a woman's sensitivity and intuition make her more receptive to connection with the other side.

The first 'sighting' was reported to me by email about a month after my husband passed away, and it came from one of his former students. I have indicated how well liked Noel was, and this was especially true of his students. After his death became known, the messages I received from his former students were many, long and glowing tributes to the man who had shown compassion for those who didn't "get chemistry" as well as those who went on to Ivy League schools, majored in science, and used their notes from his class to succeed. However, the message pertinent to this conversation came from a former student who was probably in one of Noel's classes at the beginning of his teaching career in the early 60's This man wrote to tell me that he had had a very unusual experience. He was riding his motorcycle one morning, and he suddenly felt a presence riding with him...about this he was adamant. According to Jim, Noel identified himself and seemed to be enjoying the ride, and Jim said it brought him a lot of pleasure to know his science teacher was with him. Jim had no knowledge of my experiences at that time, my point being he was a voice out of Noel's past who simply wrote to me of something that happened to him.

The second male figure with whom Noel made contact is a fellow educator who taught with him in the science department and has been a long-time friend of our family. Don has always been a morning person, and as such was in the habit of arriving at school very early, long before the students. On this particular morning he arrived at six-fifteen. As he sat at his computer, typing a letter to those who had recently chaperoned the prom, he found himself thinking about the fact that Noel and I had helped with this activity for so many years. Don went on to say he began to think about Noel's death, which had been a very emotional time for him. Before long he said what he felt was simply a presence, something he attempted to ignore. While he continued to work at the computer, the feeling became so intense he started to talk to Noel. Within moments, on the other side of the room, an adding machine Don had used for years started up-spontaneously. He went over to see what was happening and observed the machine had produced a slip of paper containing six vertical zeroes, each with a space between them. Our friend was shaken by this, adding he stood there for a while, not knowing what to do. He finally went back to his computer, at which point the adding machine started up again, and when he returned to it, it had printed the number 232. This was Noel's room number for as long as he taught in that building, twenty-eight years. My friend hurriedly finished his letter and took it down the hall to the copier. He noticed the hall was cold, but when he reached the entrance to room 232, he said he experienced a strong sensation of heat entering through his feet, washing over him, and leaving, finally, through his head. He added that from a scientific point of view, it seemed like a flow of energy that made him shiver convulsively when it happened. This is a man who has his doctorate and is very much a scientific thinker. Don concluded his story by saying later in the day he tried to make the adding machine produce the same configuration of zeroes as it had in the morning. No matter what he did, the tape showed 0.0 as opposed to the six single vertical zeroes with spaces between each entry.

And the meaning of the six zeroes? Don asked me how old Noel was when he passed away, and I answered, "Sixty." I wish I could say he retained the machine tape, but he did not. However, I have no doubt that something happened to Don in his room that morning. While no one but he knows exactly what it was, I believe because he was thinking intently about Noel, it is very possible those thoughts became a summons of sorts, and Noel, as he did so often in life, responded.

I have discussed MD's experiences, first during the morning hours when Noel passed away, and later on our back porch when she arrived for her visit. Both Ann and Linda knew Noel, but unlike Sherrill and Don, they weren't especially close to him. Nevertheless, all of these people had a connection to my husband and me, and all shared the common bond of sadness when he passed away. Thus I find the credibility of their stories very plausible. Perhaps the strangest of all contacts, however, was reported by a woman I know only through the Internet, someone who never knew Noel.

When I first reported the passing of my husband to the Chronic Lymphocytic Leukemia List, numerous messages of comfort and good wishes came my way. After all, these messages came from people knew the terror of the disease and recognized at some time they, as well as their loved ones might experience the same horror I had gone through. One woman, Patricia, wrote to tell me that despite the fact that she had never met Noel, she had the sense he was around her, helping her through some very tough times when she was seeing her oncologist. At this point, I want to make it clear I had not shared any of the aforementioned experiences with people on the List.

Patricia sent an e-mail to me one day saying, "I thought of you two weeks ago when I was looking for some pictures I had developed. I picked up an envelope and the name on it was Noel. I thought of your wonderful husband right away, and I continued searching through the big pile when I found about five envelopes with the last name Lucas on them. I had been rather nervous about waiting for the results of my PCR test, and I had to smile when I realized someone was sending me a message to relax and let go of the anxiety that was eating me up at the moment. My eyes are tearing up just thinking about it."

One of the best encounters by someone other than me was one that was downright funny, and it came from none other than my older granddaughter, Alex. She was almost five years of age at the time, but I have come to accept what so many mediums contend: children and animals are the most receptive to the presence of spirits around us. What follows certainly supports that idea, and even dark humor has its place, or so I learned when I was driving my new car of four months with my granddaughter in the back.

"Nana, did Pop Pop ever ride in this car?" Alex asked this question from her car seat behind me. I answered that she knew he hadn't because the car had been purchased just a few months before, after he had gone to heaven She replied very seriously, "Well, he's riding in it now!" and with that she leaned over the side of her car seat, grabbed the seat belt, and said, "Buckle up, Pop Pop. It's the safe thing." As I recounted this incident later to my friends, I told them in explicit language why I came close to pulling the car to the side of the road. Seeing her grandmother with wet pants isn't an image I wanted Alex to retain.

On one occasion when my daughters, my son-in-law and I were playing cards at my breakfast room table, I noticed that Stephanie's dog, Ella, lay staring into my darkened dining room. Suddenly she began to growl, a low throaty growl that she often emitted when she saw something in the dark. She continued fussing until we finally got up, turned on the lights, and began searching for whatever might be causing the dog to behave this way. I thought perhaps she had seen a palmetto bug or maybe even a mouse, but Stephanie assured me that had that been the case, Ella would have pounced on either one. Instead, she simply lay in the same place, her growls tapering off to low-pitched whines. Finally, we went back to our card game. The dog remained very still, staring at the same spot, and growling periodically for another five minutes. This could have been caused by a number of things, but in the back of my mind was the knowledge that no one liked to get together for a game of cards with his family more than Noel. While the rest of us were engrossed with the hands dealt to us, Ella may very well have seen the one looking on that evening!

When my friend Linda wrote to me on another occasion, she mentioned something that caused me to think more intently about Noel's communication with others. In her letter she said, "It is truly a testimony to your love for Noel and to his for you that he attempts to contact others." Christine Wicker also addressed this, and what she said supports Linda's contention although neither woman knows the other. Christine said, "It seems to me the fact that other people have received messages from and about Noel, and these confirmations are coming from different people in different ways, is impressive, especially because none of it is connected in any way. I wonder why you have had so much confirmation. Maybe it is because Noel wants you to write your book. Maybe because the two of you were so close, it is easier for him to break through. I don't think I've ever heard a story with some many things adding up."

I believe the quote by Maya Angelou appearing at the beginning of this chapter is worthy of repeating. She claims, "A great soul serves everyone all the time. A great soul never dies. It brings us together again and again." I know my husband was a special human being, and I believe his soul lives on because so many people from different places, different backgrounds, and different ages seem to have connected with him after he transitioned to the other side. It is particularly comforting to know communication after his passing hasn't been limited to me. Nor do I feel the need to rationalize the possibility that acute sadness clouded my ability to see what was real. I did not seek out these stories, nor did I pose questions that might have led the storyteller in a direction I wanted to go. Instead, they came to me. Through his contact with others, I received much-needed validation for the many times I prayed I was not losing my mind. Indeed, my husband's passing brought together a confluence of individuals whose affirmation of his very real contacts made my journey so much easier, and for that I am especially grateful.

TWENTY-TWO

other women, different
stories, same conclusion

Chance is always powerful. Let your hook be always cast;
in the pool where you least expect it, there will be a fish.
-Ovid

Every time I let myself think about the number of people who confirmed my belief Noel was sending messages from the other side, I am astounded all over again. My granddaughters had indicated in their childlike ways that Noel had shown himself to them. My younger daughter, Stephanie, had many dreams she feels certain were the result of her Dad's communication, and on one occasion she attributes his presence to alerting her to a potentially serious situation. One night in the fall, after she had gone to bed, she awoke around two o'clock and felt an intense cold. Opening her bedroom door and moving into the hall, she discovered her front door standing wide open. She has always kept that door locked because she uses the kitchen door consistently. Feelings of concern quickly wakened her because she feared someone may have entered her house. However, as she moved into her living room where a lamp was still lighted, she discovered she had forgotten to extinguish a candle when she went to bed, and the wax had puddled onto the wood mantle. Stephanie will assure you her Dad was instrumental in wakening her so that she might make the discovery before it became an emergency. Cold alone may not have done it, but an open front door that was always locked left no doubt for her.

Certainly the number of my friends who experienced contact from Noel was stunning in itself, people who in many cases never met one another. However, in the two to three years after Noel passed away, I found myself engaged with people I did not know, women whose husbands had died within the same time frame as mine, women who didn't know me but were willing to share their stories, clinging, as I did, to a need for reassurance that others had experienced the same kind of connection.

You can surely imagine how reluctant I was to broach the topic of communication from deceased loved ones with women who had lost their husbands. Many of these widows were in the early stages of grief and had been impacted, just as I was, by the unimaginable. To approach them with questions they could consider intrusive, not to mention bizarre, required a delicacy I don't pretend to possess. Yet feeling so positive about my own experiences and the insights I had gained, I longed to tell anyone who was floundering that there is real hope for contact. While I knew I was unable provide instructions on how they might bring this about, I wanted to encourage them to try to reach some place of inner calm, because this just might help them to become more receptive. Nevertheless, I knew that despite the fact I often want to shout it from the hills, I had to tread lightly.

One of my best resources was the CLL web site I have spoken of before. At no time did I ever barge online to ask whether or not those who had lost someone had rediscovered that person through communication with the other side. I was never *that* desperate for reinforcement. However, over the course of time, I remained a part of this group, and, occasionally, the topic would drift toward the spiritual. When that happened I often wrote privately to the individual who had posted on the subject. I was surprised by the number of people who responded, every bit as eager as I to discuss the implications of spiritual connection.

Just as I was struck by the number of people with whom Noel communicated, so was I surprised by the stories told by widows who had experiences similar mine. These stories came directly, and sometimes indirectly, from folks on the CLL List for which I have so much respect. I had watched people tell their stories on *Crossing Over*, and I read books about communication with souls from the other side. But here were very credible people, women as ordinary as I, who were telling me of incidents that would be considered by skeptics to be as unbelievable as I considered mine to be at first! They were not the focus of a television show or featured in a magazine or book that relies on sensationalism. These were individuals who, like me, suddenly found themselves in the middle of something unfathomable, and were as perplexed as I by what was happening. Without exception, every woman came to accept her experience was real, just as I had.

What follows are stories that were provided, initially, through a second party. I asked the tellers if they would return to the widow in question and seek permission for me to contact them directly so I could listen to their versions independently and avoid misinterpretation. These are the stories of three women who don't know one another, nor do they know *about* one another. Furthermore, they live about as far apart as possible, though all live in the United States. At their request, I have not used their real names.

I first heard about Elaine through an e-mail friend who posts to the Chronic Lymphocytic Leukemia website. My friend told me that Elaine's husband had passed away several weeks before and indicated that she thought it would help if I were to talk to her. The story I learned was this: two weeks after Elaine's husband passed away her phone rang one morning, and when she answered it, there was no one on the other end of the line. She didn't think much about it beyond the probability that someone had dialed the wrong number, so she simply hung up. Shortly thereafter, the phone rang a second time, and the result was the same. It was then that Elaine dialed *69 to get the number of the caller, only to discover the number consisted of just four digits instead of the usual seven. These four numbers were 4444, a number she recognized immediately as the pin number her husband always used for banking and other business transactions. In all the time Elaine has used *69, she never experienced the appearance of anything other than a standard phone number, and she feels certain her husband was responsible for this connection.

The second woman to experience contact had many stories to tell, but the one that struck me as the most forceful occurred the summer following her husband's passing in February. Justine told me she had decided to host a cookout despite the fact that she was feeling depressed. Knowing her sons were worried about her, Justine felt this might be a way to reassure them. She continued her story by talking about one of the 'toys' her husband had purchased before his illness became debilitating, a car that could be started by remote control from inside the house. During the party one of her sons came to her and asked why the car's engine was running. Justine replied she had not started it, but perhaps someone else had. Still very much in the throes of grief, she was doing all she could to cope with the party and didn't think much about the car other than to tell her son to turn the motor off. About an hour later, Justine was near the garage and heard what she knew was the running motor of the car. She went to her son and asked why he hadn't turned off the motor as she asked him to do, and he assured her that he had. It was then that she knew that her husband had been around the gathering all evening, and this was his way of letting her know. Rather than being frightened, Justine said the incident helped her get through the rest of the evening.

The third story was told to me by a widow, Laura. After losing her husband, Laura continued to frequent the club where they had both played tennis on a regular basis. One day as she entered the ladies' locker room, she noticed a piece of crumpled paper on the floor, and her first thought was someone had missed the wastebasket that was close by. She said ordinarily, as a matter of course, she would have picked it up and disposed of it. Instead, she went in to finish dressing and didn't think any more about the paper until she came out into the common area of the locker again. The paper was still lying on the floor. She told me she almost ignored it a second time, but finally she picked it up. She unfolded the scrap of paper to find a single word written on it. The word was the nickname that her deceased husband had been given by three male friends, and only they and she knew the name, because her husband disliked it so much.

As I listened to these stories, I could envision the jolt each of these women must have felt, but I could also sense the euphoria they must have experienced when the reality dawned upon each that she had been given something special. My own emotions escalated tenfold when I listened to their stories: happiness for the reassurance each had been given and immense gratitude that I had found additional solid ground upon which I could stand and overcome my incessant need to find what many would term 'rational' reasons for my own experiences.

I am certain I will never divest myself entirely of some skepticism, and in many respects this is healthy. But because so much has happened to me and to others in whom I place a great deal of trust, I don't question everything the way I used to do. There is nothing to be gained from doing so, and there is so much more to be lost.

TWENTY-THREE

the female factor

Women remember the first kiss, men remember the last.
-Unknown

I have to confess I used to have a tendency to mentally (and sometimes verbally) deride the exchanges I saw taking place among women. What I often observed was one female seemingly threatened by another whose only sin was that she had managed to progress up the ladder, any work-related ladder. There were times when the threatened party acted out in the form of sabotage, attempting to 'get even' for her perceived injuries. In the workplace, when a woman could often use the help of a sister, she preferred instead, for whatever reason, to gain help from a man. Whether or not she deemed it a form of weakness to ask another female for assistance is speculation, but I found myself lamenting the fact that these women were frequently their own worst enemies. I even went so far as to label this "congenital bitchery." Back then I believed too many women failed to support one another as much as they should.

Don't misunderstand me. I have always had female friends. They were a few women, with whom I enjoyed long and lasting relationships, women who often thought as I did, although we could disagree with one another without hurt feelings. Most importantly, these women enjoyed spirited exchanges. Yet the truth is, when I was a young mother, I did not seek out women who chose to talk exclusively about formula and diapers. I craved deeper discussion and often found myself preferring my male friends for reinforcement.

That said, I have made a one-hundred-eighty degree turn and am now quick to acknowledge that exactly the opposite takes over when loss and the accompanying grief are tossed into the mix. In truth my experiences with my friends after Noel's passing shredded the blinders of my tunnel vision regarding women helping other women.

When I was doing research for my book, a friend sent me an article by Jean Houston which appeared in a *Brookhaven Women in Science* (BWIS) publication. What follows are portions of the article. As you read these excerpts, think of them in terms of your grieving process, and pay particular attention to the salient point made at the end.

Women respond to stress differently than men do. Fortunately, we also have a better way to fight it: each other. Friendships between women are special. They shape who we are and who we are yet to be. They soothe our tumultuous inner world, fill the emotional gaps in our marriage, and help us remember who we really are. But they may do even more. Scientists now suspect that hanging out with our friends can actually counteract the kind of stomach-quivering stress most of us experience on a daily basis.

A landmark UCLA study suggests that women respond to stress with a cascade of brain chemicals that cause us to make and maintain friendships with other women. It's a stunning finding that has turned five decades of stress research-most of it on men-upside down.

"Until this study was published, scientists generally believed that when people experience stress, they trigger a hormonal cascade that revs the body to either stand and fight or flee as fast as possible," explains Laura Cousino Klein, PhD, assistant professor of bio-behavioral health at Pennsylvania State University. It's an ancient survival mechanism left over from the time we were chased across the planet by saber-toothed tigers. Now the researchers suspect that women have a larger behavioral repertoire than just "fight or flight."

In fact, says Dr. Klein, it seems that when the hormone oxytocin is released as part of the stress response in a woman, it buffers the fight or flight response and encourages her to tend children and gather with other women instead. When she actually engages in this tending or befriending, studies suggest that more oxytocin is released, which further counters stress and produces a calming effect.

came to my home in South Carolina. We still connect periodically, and when we talk, it is as though we have been friends forever. I believe grief has a rather unusual power to bond women in a unique and lasting way.

While my earlier contention used to be that women fall woefully short in providing support for one another, my experience after losing Noel turned that supposition on its head. I discovered the fallacy of my thinking and came to recognize what a treasure I was given. Widows who don't have close female friends need to cultivate such relationships. As Jean Houston suggests, this can be life-altering and perhaps life-saving.

TWENTY-FOUR

there's the love, and there's the sex

"I knew how good it could be to fall in love. I really loved Charles. After he died, though, I never tried to find love again. I think I was afraid of failing. Isn't that pathetic? I was too afraid to go after the best thing I ever found in this life."
-James Patterson
Four Blind Mice

There was a time when my younger daughter attempted to convince me of the merits of having a dog in my life. It would provide company for me, she insisted, to have a live creature in the house. Then she came forth with what I'm sure she thought was a major selling point when she said, "Come on, Mom, it would be nice for you to have a dog in your bed at night!" I rolled my eyes, and my response was one that no child ever wants to hear her mother say. I told her to trust me it wasn't a dog I needed in my bed! Then it became her turn to roll her eyes, this exaggerated gesture accompanied by a groan that fell somewhere between incredulity and disgust. We both laughed, somewhat nervously I might add; she giggled for one reason, and I for another.

The more I thought about it, the more I came to accept the implication of my daughter's words. I did need someone in my bed, and without a doubt sex plays a role in that need. The 'good-girls-don't-do-it-until-they-are-married' axiom that was pounded into me as I was growing up, at long last, had disappeared from this realistic widow's lexicon; yet I still believe there is more to it than raw desire. I needed the comfort of knowing someone was there when I went to sleep at night. There were times when I placed a pillow at my back so that when I drifted off to sleep and entered the netherworld where reality and fantasy became a finely blended elixir, I felt something nestled against my body I hoped would trick my mind and let my imagination take over.

I am a product of the free-love sixties, but while I have come a long way in shedding my hang-ups regarding the prerequisite of a marriage certificate, I still have trouble hopping into bed with someone as a matter of course at the end of a night out. Furthermore, I don't think that's a bad thing. One evening, as I sat with my daughters on the porch, again consuming copious amounts of wine, I divulged to them that I had come to my marriage night a virgin, despite seven years of dating their father. After many minutes of uproarious, non-stop laughter, they concurred that I was, indeed, the eighth wonder of the world. I couldn't decide if they were incredulous, embarrassed, or they simply didn't believe me. In fact, there was a very long time after Noel passed away that I couldn't imagine making love to any man other than my late husband; thus I knew I would have a major problem on my hands if I ever dated again.

The bed at night is perhaps one of the loneliest places a widow can find herself. A friend, who lost her husband a year before I did, told me that she could not stand to wake up and look across the bed to where he once slept, so she chose to sleep on his side. Initially I thought that seemed a bit absurd and it would never work for me, but once I started my pillow routine, I came to realize every woman must use to her advantage any ploy to make her day-to-day, or more accurately, night-to-night, life less painful.

At one point I thought to myself, "Perhaps what I need right now more than anything is a companion." I have always been a people person, one who feels best when interacting with others. I missed that aspect of my life when I was at home alone, especially in the evening. It isn't that Noel and I spent every moment talking; if anything, we spent a lot of time in easy quiet. But the joking and the banter, along with the serious talks, were a very special part of our relationship, and there was a huge hole in my life when I no longer enjoyed such intimate exchange. I came to appreciate how exquisite the deep resonance of a male voice is when it was no longer commonplace in my home.

Then there is the matter of loving deeply again. A friend who knew both my husband and me for a number of years told me shortly after Noel passed away that she imagined I would have a difficult time dating, because no one would ever measure up to all my husband had been for me. Romantic love was basic to my life from the time I was fifteen, and I had to get past the very romantic (read unrealistic) idea there could be but one meaningful love in a person's life. As the years stretched from three to five to seven, and I continued my journey without the only love I had known, I began to find myself more receptive to having someone else share with me what life has to offer.

Many who have experienced a second love say it will happen when you least expect it. Furthermore, those same people insist a second love is never meant to replace the first. There continues to be comfort for me in that thought, because after several years of solitude, I am at last in a place that lies well beyond the self-torture and guilt I inflicted upon myself when I tried earlier to justify bringing another man into my life.

When television actress Mariska Hargitay was interviewed, she commented on her first marriage, entered into when she was forty, and her thoughts not only provided an interesting perspective but also shed some much-needed light on the place where I found myself. The words are encouraging, not only for people whose first marriage comes later in life, but also for those of us hoping to establish a new love life as well. She said, "I had to find out where I was going first, before I could determine who was going with me." Any widow struggling to find her way to the place where she can make clear-headed decisions, especially about new love, can readily appreciate this insight.

In Mitch Albom's book, *The Five People You Meet in Heaven*, there is a passage that we who have been widowed should read over and over until we finally get it. The words are simple yet eloquent, and I believe if we can accept the content of these lines as true, we will be better able to withstand our loss and also cope with our need for the human touch and the ensuing love that touch may produce. When Eddie finally meets his wife in heaven, the following conversation takes place:

"I never wanted anyone else," he said quietly.

"I know," she said.

"I was still in love with you."

"I know." She nodded. "I felt it."

"Here?" he asked.

"Even here," she said smiling. "That's how strong lost love can be."

I cried the first time I read this because I could almost hear my husband and I having such a conversation. Every bit of me wants to believe, without question, that Noel can still feel my love for him wherever he may be. The passage resonates deeply within me, and I know somewhere in time and space my husband must understand I have received the message. But I also know that he would not want me to go through the rest of my life without the love and support of another man.

My feelings for Noel were a huge force in my life, and I believe he cared for me just as deeply. One time I wrote an article for our school newspaper in which I gave him the credit he so justly deserved for one of my successful projects. I referred to him as "the wind beneath my wings," and even now, there is still no better way to describe what his presence meant. His passing and the communications he sent to me from the other side seemed to move me along the continuum of self-discovery, a gossamer thread that refused to break. If, after all, everything comes down to the single word *love*, then it was Noel's continuing love for me that propelled me along the path I chose. At times I was capable of soaring above the path; other times it was necessary to glide close to its surface. But always it was the love that provided the impetus for me to keep moving.

So how does one juxtapose the loving relationship that once drove every aspect of her life beside the need for male companionship that may become love, given time? Some claim the best testament to a strong, loving marriage is the willingness to try it again, despite the apprehension. If, as folks say, it will happen when you least expect it, then you don't have control over the situation anyway. On most occasions when this dilemma overtook my thinking, I simply chose to pull a Scarlett O'Hara and say, "I'll think about that tomorrow." This approach worked well for me as I dealt with many issues that widowhood produces. I continue to believe that out there somewhere is a larger plan being put into action, and my job is to exercise patience, something I've never done particularly well. But I am working on it.

TWENTY-FIVE

don't go where the guilt lies in wait

*Guilt is the least valuable and most
destructive of human emotions!*
-Anonymous

It seems entirely appropriate to follow a chapter devoted to sex, or the possibility of sex, with one that focuses on guilt. After all, as a young woman who came of age in the early sixties, I discovered guilt was the handiest tool a parent could use. My mother made it very clear to me from the time she thought I might know anything about 'the deed' that if I were to become pregnant, my dad would "kill both of us." Those were her exact words. Because my father had a fiery temper, I never chose to question Mom's declaration. Later I saw the ploy for what it was: fear combined with guilt provided my mother with absolute power, a cudgel that was wielded with ease and resulted in success, at least from her perspective. It wasn't so great for my psyche, however, and as a result, I was never able to completely rid myself of the big G, especially when it dealt with anything pleasurable.

To this day if there is a chance that guilt might be attached to any aspect of my existence, I will somehow find a way to strap it on my back and carry it along with me. I have come to accept after some time spent in therapy that guilt and the behavior that results is learned; yet somehow I have never been able to unlearn it, despite years of trying. So when I spoke to my friend, Ann, who told me how she had held her comatose husband in her arms and sang to him as he left this life, I felt terrible that I hadn't done the same.

I return in my mind to the way Stephanie and I spent our last hours with Noel, talking to him and making every effort to see that he left this life with dignity and love. My dear friend, Nancy, who was a vital part of my support system (along with her husband, Walt), had volunteered with Hospice for years. She told me later how amazed she was by our instincts, and she insisted we had put into action much of what Hospice care advocates under these circumstances. She added this usually comes about after a great deal of training. I can truthfully say when I was confronted with the inevitability of Noel's death that evening, I had no idea how I would make it through the next five minutes much less the night that lay ahead. There was no plan, only the sense that I was living someone else's nightmare.

One would think my friend's reinforcement should have been sufficient to keep my guilt at bay. Yet I found my mind constantly replaying the last hours of Noel's life in his hospital room, and every time, I would envision Ann holding her husband. This resulted in repeated feelings of failure. Why didn't I get into the bed, take him in my arms, and hold him at the time when he probably needed me most? Was it the breathing tube that held me back? I have asked myself a thousand times whether or not I was terrified by thoughts of touching near-death itself. If I were that cowardly, how could I live with myself? I tormented myself so many times with questions like this, questions for which there are no clear answers.

The fact is that I probably did experience some elemental fear of the death process. I know I held his hands, and I pray I kissed him often although in truth my recollection of having done so is vague. I have come to accept that maybe the blur of this awful time is a blessing that, thankfully, my brain has seen fit to bestow upon me. There is something to be said for the inability to replay every numbing minute I had to endure when part of me was dying as well. Watching your life dwindle to nothing isn't something you should want to recall in detail. Yet when these thoughts would rise unbidden, I asked myself repeatedly whether or not I really rose to the occasion as valiantly as others must surely have done. When self-doubt taunted me like a feared specter, I was overwhelmed by sadness. Early in my grieving, it was during those times of guilt that I came closest to not wanting to go on.

I know in my heart there were no unresolved issues between Noel and me at the time of his passing, because we had seventeen months from the time he was diagnosed until his death to work through any minor issues of an otherwise rock solid relationship. This sustained me ninety-nine percent of the time. But when that old learned habit reared its hoary head, the remaining one percent kicked in with vengeance.

There were times I also questioned how I managed to reach a state of calm early on, when in my heart I still felt the crushing loss of the person who was central to my life. Was there something the matter with me that permitted this apparently together woman on the outside to coalesce so seamlessly with the one who was broken inside? Was I living some kind of schizophrenic existence? In this respect I was, once again, my own worst enemy.

Eventually I came to appreciate that if I did not get a handle on this self-inflicted torment, it would destroy the truth and integrity of all I had done for the person whose life meant more to me than my own. I remembered the time when Noel told a friend that he could never have asked for a better patient advocate than I was for him when he needed me most. Thus I knew that I had to stop degrading my husband's sincere appreciation for my efforts with my self-induced guilt trips. Somewhere I read, "Don't take guilt trips. Take a trip to the mall, to the next county, to a foreign country, but NOT to where the guilt is." Ultimately I came to recognize this was a much healthier approach, one I finally accepted, at least most of the time.

Earlier in the book I noted that widowhood is not the same for any two women because of the differences and complexities in marriages and personalities. That same axiom applies to feelings of guilt, because no two people respond in the same way to stress and the anguish it often produces. I found I needed to remove myself from the mindset of 'what if' and acknowledge I had done the best I could do at the time. I would suggest to any widow that she grant herself the same peace if she is overwhelmed by any feelings that resemble guilt. Read and reread the anonymous quote appearing at the beginning of this chapter. Copy it on paper and stick it to your bathroom mirror so that every morning you are reminded that what you are doing to yourself is destructive and lacks any redeeming value. Be kind to yourself, and know it helps those around you as well.

Fortunately these questions of guilt and self-doubt that held me captive in the early months of my widowhood began to fade. As I continued to make my way through the labyrinth of grief, sometimes I hit a wall and shut down entirely, but more often than not, I simply detoured. Those amazing messages that kept coming from the other side, as well as support from the people around me, eased my guilt and aided my mourning in ways that I am sure I don't fully understand to this day. What I do recognize is this: when we lose someone whose presence was integral to our very existence, most of us will question why it had to happen. In doing so we often turn that question inward, consciously or subconsciously wondering if the loss had something to do with our own shortcomings. I feel confident in saying to any widow, without qualification, it didn't. Furthermore I would admonish you not to go there. It helps no one, least of all the grieving spouse who is struggling to retool her sense of self. Give yourself a fair chance to heal without the burden of feeling any guilt.

TWENTY-SIX

why *not* me?

*I think somehow we learn who we really
are, then live with that decision.*
-Eleanor Roosevelt

Now that you have been soundly lectured on what *not* to do regarding guilt, that if you cozy up to guilt it is self-destructive, I want to turn your attention to another trap widows often fall into, one of self-pity and questioning why this had to happen to you. It is easy to succumb to the "why me?" syndrome when you are plunged into the depression of loss; so often it rises up to nip at you like a tenacious mosquito on your sweaty arm. You rationalize that you have been a good person and you don't purposely hurt anyone. Any woman who has strong religious faith may find that faith shaken by her loss, and may fear that, unlike life before the bomb was dropped, her belief may never be as deep as it once was.

How many times have you heard someone say, "It will just take time to get over your loss?" They mean well, but they are clueless. Time is a very different concept for each of us, especially as we walk through the density of sorrow. When you lose the person you love, your entire life is derailed, and getting the train back on track is no small task. Even more daunting is deciding in which direction the train should go. Thus it is very easy to question why you were singled out for something this horrific. However, I need to point out how letting the "why me?" question overtake you can ultimately become a destructive force.

The first few months after Noel passed away, I fluctuated between the very high and the miserably low. On one hand I was buoyed by sheer adrenaline and bounced along in the rough waters of grief in spite of myself. People would ask with genuine concern how I was faring, and I would respond that I was doing very well, thank you. And I was- at the exact moment I was speaking. Yes, I had my serious crying sessions that would drag me down for an entire morning. I remember one in particular when I ran to the mahogany box containing Noel's ashes, took it from the shelf, and sat on the floor behind a large wing back chair in the living room, keening as I rocked back and forth. This is hardly a picture of someone with well-honed coping skills. Yet gradually I seemed to bounce back from these early emotional maelstroms, and I managed to move forward with determination. Only when I let myself reflect on the unalterable fact that Noel was gone from me physically *forever* did life become unbearable, and the suffocating "why me?" dropped upon me like a soggy woolen blanket.

Fortunately, as those communications I thought might be coming from my husband occurred more frequently, and I found myself in periods of introspection, I came to accept a greater revelation, one that began to extinguish the red-hot flame of pain and guide me to a calmer blue flickering of warmth. Over time I discovered that *forever* does, indeed, play a part in our lives. The more I dreamed, the more signs I saw, the more frequently I felt Noel's presence around me, the more crystalline this realization became. Noel would certainly be gone from me forever *physically,* but his spiritual presence would be mine for as long as I let myself be receptive to it; *forever* if that was my choice. In many respects this became the only control I had over the anxiety that otherwise might have consumed me.

"Nana, did Pop Pop die forever?" When my three-year-old granddaughter, Sydney, asked this question, we were riding in my golf cart. The question pulled me up short for many reasons, not the least of which was the source, because Sydney was only nine months old when Noel passed away. Before I had a chance to answer, Alexandra jumped into the conversation, informing me she had told Sydney that even though she couldn't see Pop Pop, he was still around her forever. Ah, the sweet wisdom of young children. So there it was again, the quandary of defining "forever." I walked a fine line with my granddaughters in my efforts to honestly answer their questions about Noel's passing. However, 'death' and 'forever' were concepts too confounding for me to explain. Thus I was grateful for Alex's willingness to assume the role of the well-informed big sister and take me off the hook.

"Why *me*?" Eventually I discovered the answer to that question by asking yet another question, "Why *not* me?" What made me so special that I merited exclusion from the legions of widows who are now, have been, and will continue to be? This became especially clear after 9/11 when I thought about all the women who had lost their husbands or significant others, not just those whose stories were attractive to the media, but the hundreds of others whose loss went unrecorded except in their own hellish reality. Thus I came to understand, as I tried to tease out answers and arrive at conclusions, I first had to get past the always-present 'why me.' I needed to recognize that feeling for what it is, one with no small measure of self-pity.

Falling prey to this consuming question, while understandable, accomplishes very little. By exchanging a very sad and pointless approach for one that included opening myself (read this to mean letting go), I was able to move past 'why me'. In part this can be accomplished when widows learn to appreciate themselves more; however, that is a serious challenge for the woman who feels as though half of her very being has been hacked away and discarded. In the words of Theodore Isaac Ruben, "Compassion for myself is the most powerful healer of them all." While sympathy for and understanding of others is hugely important, it is the compassion for the self that will move a woman forward.

I was blessed with incredible love and support from my husband during the time we had together. As I grew older and complained about the added weight, the sagging breasts, and the wrinkles that took my forehead hostage, he would always say, "Hey, Babe, it's the body I love." Sadly, I believed I might never again hear those words directed toward me so convincingly. By the same token, I knew that I had to stop looking in the mirror, expecting to see the reflection of a widow, and instead seek out and accept myself as an enduring woman who had met grief head-on and emerged from tragedy a stronger person. To do otherwise would be to cast aside all the effort Noel so consistently put forth to make me feel good about myself.

A big part of moving beyond grief and into the comfort of determination and self-love is acceptance of our new persona. It is true that we are widows, but we are so much more if we just let ourselves be. Women in our position must attempt to become a subtle blend of what we were and what we can be. After all, we gave and received love in a relationship that can never be replicated. The same skills created and nurtured by that love will help us in so many ways if we just let them come to the surface. Giving affection to those in need, those who probably were never fortunate enough to experience what we were given for so long, is surely a way to hoist ourselves out of self-pity. I found volunteering my time was very rewarding, and the following account of something that happened during a volunteer session underscores just how great the reward might be.

At my daughter's suggestion, I decided to join a bereavement group sponsored by our local hospice that met once a week, six weeks in all. The participants were all very kind, somewhat bewildered by what had befallen them, and basically seeking the same thing: other folks who understood what they were going through. At the conclusion of the last session, the hospice facilitator asked me stay. She wanted to know whether or not I would participate in an upcoming program that sent hospice representatives into the schools to work with kids who had lost someone close or had a relative who was dying. She knew I had taught high school, and thought this might be something I could easily do. I told her I really had no desire to go back into a school setting, so she countered by asking if I thought I could work with a child one-on-one. I gave it some consideration over the next few days and came to the conclusion this experience might provide another dimension for my own grieving. I was an adult who was having a difficult time dealing with death. What must it be like for a child? I had some apprehension, fearing how fragile a young person in this painful state might be, but something told me I should try.

When I met Olivia (not her real name), who was twelve at the time, she was a mix of so many of the emotions I had experienced. I immediately recognized the belligerence of 'why me?' that she used in an attempt to mask her distress and confusion. Olivia had lost her father the month before, and she really didn't want to talk about it. Eventually we got past her reticence, and over the next few weeks she began to open up. One day she asked me, "If I tell you something that happened the day after my dad died, something pretty crazy, will you think I'm nuts?" I assured her I would be the last person to think that, knowing what I had experienced after Noel died. Of course, I hadn't told her about my experiences; it simply wouldn't have been appropriate. Olivia went on to say she had been sitting by herself at the picnic table outside of her house when she felt something beside her. She added, "I had my head down on the table, and I was crying. When I lifted my head, I saw Dad sitting there like he used to do when we talked, and he told me not to cry. He said he was fine, and I should be brave." She paused here and said, "I bet you do think I'm crazy." I started to laugh, and I said, "Oh, my sweet child, if you are crazy, then so am I." I went on to describe a couple of the incidents regarding Noel's communication to me, and Olivia's face revealed what could only be described as genuine relief. Little did this child realize that just as my stories provided help for her anxiety, so did her experience give me added support in my quest for answers so that I could move on. I could only hope the exchange between Olivia and me helped her forward progress as well.

This having been said, there can be a downside to the 'moving on' process. Unfortunately, as we begin to navigate this difficult transformation, the subtle expectation on the part of others is that we should also try to shut the door, albeit gently, on our past. It is a dilemma made worse today because we are people who thrive on buzzwords. In the realm of bereavement, I submit the word "closure" is the word of the day, or at least it was when my grief was relatively new. For some reason, people who had lost a person central to their lives were expected to work diligently at attaining closure. Regardless of how advocates of this termination process worked around it, the word conveyed to me the need to tie up my emotions in a neat package and store them on a shelf. Maybe I was missing something, but I had no desire for closure. This was the most life-altering experience of my existence How was I to terminate something of this magnitude, acting as though it had never happened? It didn't mean that I choose to dwell morbidly or wallow in my grief, but I certainly could not see myself shutting down on the subject entirely. Even today, every time I look at either of my daughters or my granddaughters, I see Noel. They don't necessarily look like him, but they embody much of what he was, so unless I banish them from my sight, there can be no closure.

What defines closure? Does it mean getting a grip and moving on, and if so, then how does one go about accomplishing this seemingly impossible task? Having read about the stages of grief, I began questioning myself when I failed to experience the anger stage. I can say with all honesty that I have never felt any real rage for Noel's leaving me, so it was difficult to associate that emotion with my loss. It was true that I was disappointed that he left so early in life, but I don't believe that included anger directed toward him or God, for that matter. I came to see that if I had to experience each and every stage of grief so that I could attain closure, I was in trouble. I have yet to feel anger toward anyone for Noel's passing, especially Noel. Over time I arrived at the conclusion that as I became more spiritually attuned to the connections I made, closure was the last thing I wanted. And so, my fellow travelers, I strongly suggest ignoring that prescriptive. Having retired from public school teaching after thirty-two years, I can tell you that there is no group of people more compelled to regularly change the verbiage of their profession than educators. When I left the classroom in 1997, 'paradigm' was the hot-button word, and it didn't make for better teachers any more than the word 'closure' will help to promote merrier widows!

"Why me?" Perhaps the answer rests with the very simple notion that this is part of my own soul's work, a chance for me to become the person I am meant to become. Even if this is inaccurate, it isn't a bad place to start looking for an answer. A quote tacked at the end of a recent e-mail I received explains it fairly well. It said, "If God brings you to it, he will bring you through it." Please don't construe this as a gospel message; by now you know that isn't who I am. However, there is a great deal of truth to this statement, and every widow should repeat it to herself when things look like they won't get any better.

PART FOUR

The devil whispered in my ear,
"You're not strong enough to withstand the storm."
Today I whispered in the devil's ear, "I am the storm."
-Anonymous

TWENTY-SEVEN

cast your spell upon me one more time: lily dale, take three

This world is not the conclusion: a sequel stands beyond.
-Emily Dickinson

June 29, 2004. Once again, my friend MD and I were traveling together to Lily Dale on an afternoon that was sunny and cool for late June, even in Pennsylvania. I had agreed to a day trip this time with no overnight stay at the Takei home. Before leaving I had a good heart-to-heart with myself and sternly emphasized in this one-person conversation the fact that I could not expect this trip to replicate the two that had preceded it. Sound familiar? Nothing is more certain than change, and I had made up my mind not to delude myself into thinking otherwise. As we neared the turn into the place I had come to think of as The Land of Oz, there was no breathless anticipation or sense of the unexpected just around the corner, responses I had come to associate with my arrival at the gate of this little community.

Nevertheless, what-ifs and maybes managed to worm their way into my brain, and the effect was somewhat like that of swirling of a glass of fine wine to observe the clarity of its contents; all those alcohol-induced legs trailing down the sides of a crystal goblet, suggesting promise of the wonderful contents about to consumed.

The two previous trips and the readings that had accompanied each had occurred *exactly* two years apart, to the day. Had I subconsciously planned it that way? And now that more than a year had passed, would that be a deal breaker? Maybe Noel's spirit wasn't ready for another dramatic appearance likes those he had made before. Furthermore the mediums could very well experience an off day. After all, they, too, have the right to a headache or foggy channels. What if my senses had been overloaded by all the prior messages from 'across the way,' and what I received this time would seem drab or meaningless by comparison? What if? What if? Much like the rubber ball that is attached to a wooden paddle, my thoughts were smacking back and forth as we entered the gate.

I met with Martie first that day; after all wasn't that the established protocol? Given the fact that we hadn't seen one another for two years, we spent a little time reclaiming our friendship. I had come to trust Martie Hughes and knew she would never purposely rework any aspect of the reading. However, I still walked a fine line of healthy skepticism, and as we sat down, I made a conscious effort not to divulge information that might intrude upon or distort the message.

We started the reading shortly after my arrival, and Martie began by saying that Noel's presence wasn't as large as it had been in the past …her wording. I sat quietly, processing these words, and I assumed she meant his presence wasn't as forceful or imposing. She added that this was quite natural, and it indicated to her that I didn't need his presence as intensely as I had before. "This," she said, "is a good thing." I must have felt some resentment at what I considered presumption on her part because I remember thinking, *"Thank you, Martha Stewart, you with your good things; I happen to feel that I still rely quite heavily on my husband's presence around me."*

My face probably betrayed some distress, because she quickly added that he would always be around me when I needed him, but that I had to recognize that my needs weren't nearly as critical as they had been. Grudgingly, I agreed, but despite my attempts to feel some conviction, I felt instead something akin to disappointment; I simply couldn't help it. I could hear my daughter saying, "Don't get greedy, Mom," and I tried to hold on to her words as I anticipated what I assumed would be a letdown. If I had subconsciously harbored the thought that the third reading could still bring about something special, I had another thought coming...or did I?

Martie proceeded to tell me that Noel was spending a great deal of time around others who needed his help, in particular our granddaughter Sydney, adding that Syd was an inquisitive child whose curiosity sometimes brought her to the edge of danger. This was a huge understatement. Sydney was the child who, at two years of age, unlocked my front door, not an easy task, and wandered across the street to play with the neighbor's dog. I remember shaking with nausea when I thought about what could have happened to my granddaughter who was no more than thirty inches tall at the time. Martie finally concluded this part of the reading by saying that she could see Noel in Sydney's room at night, watching over her, and then she laughed, saying that she saw him sitting on her dresser. With that, I must break away from Martie's reading momentarily to relate a conversation I had with Sydney in May, a few weeks before I made this trip.

When I was visiting, I took Sydney to preschool one morning, and from her seat in the back of the car, she said, "Nana, why did Pop Pop have to go to heaven?" The child was prone to ask this kind of question out of the blue, and as often as it happened, she was still able to take me by surprise. I answered to the best of my ability, given that it was eight thirty in the morning, and I was surrounded by traffic. I told her that Pop Pop's body was tired and it hurt, and so he went to heaven because it wouldn't hurt there.

"And he became an angel, right?" she asked in a voice that was sweet but determined. I laughed, said yes, and then I asked whether or not she and Alex had been talking about this. It has always been Alex's contention that Noel became an angel immediately upon his entry into heaven, and of course I am still in agreement with her conjecture. Sydney acknowledged that she and her sister had been discussing Pop Pop, and then she said in a very soft voice, "You know, Nana, you can see angels at night-not in the morning when it's light but at night." *Slow the acceleration, Carol.*

"You can?" I responded, trying to keep my voice steady. "Have you seen angels at night?" I asked. Her positive response gave me the courage to add, "Have you seen Pop Pop at night?" In a very matter-of-fact tone of voice, she responded that she had. While I know that Sydney was quite young when Noel died, and her ability to recognize him may be questionable, I also know that small children have a greater capacity for understanding and accepting these things. By then we had arrived at the school. I helped Syd out of her car seat, and she joined her teacher who was waiting for a bevy of four year olds to descend, most of whom, I would guess, didn't have angels on their minds.

Now here was Martie telling me that Noel was watching over Sydney in her room at night. My heart soared, and the reality of how important this must be for Sydney was clearly a revelation. Forget *my* so-called needs.

After my trip, I went to Jennifer's home in July to celebrate Sydney's fourth birthday. One evening, after I had given her a bath, I wrapped a little pink terry robe around her, and pointing to the angel on the pocket of her robe, I asked whether or not she remembered telling me about seeing angels at night. She said she did, and when I asked her where those angels were when they came into her room, she took my hand, pulled me into the bedroom, and pointed to her dresser. Despite some early reservations about my third reading, it was a very important message. I learned that Sydney would have the benefit of her grandfather's presence around her, just not in the way we who remain here on earth might have wished.

Another aspect of Martie's reading that prompted me to reconsider my initial disappointment concerned my friend and her diagnosis. Martie told me she had a sense that Noel was helping someone else, perhaps another child, and that she saw illness as part of this relationship. "I keep getting the name Lindsay," she said and she continued to repeat the name. Finally it occurred to me that she might be referring to Linda whose letter I shared earlier. As I indicated, when Linda went to see a Native American Indian medium in Pennsylvania, she was told someone with whom she had taught and had passed away was still very much around her as she was going through this difficult time. Linda knew right away whom her medium was referencing. To my knowledge these two spiritualists have no connection with one another.

One question I had asked myself on all three visits to Lily Dale was whether or not it was a good idea to attend one reading on the heels of another. Part of me saw this as perhaps insulting to the first medium. Then again, this was probably foolish thinking; after all, two minds are better than one when seeking answers to the complexities life tosses our way. Additionally, it would not have felt right *not* to see Sherry Lee, and so because we were not staying overnight, little more than an hour later, I was sitting across from her.

This is a woman who defies the rigors that time brings to most of us; certainly she hadn't altered her looks one bit during the four years since I had contact with her. Right away she brought out her chalk and began drawing, laughing as she made broad swaths of color across the large piece of paper. It seemed she was being instructed to draw a big brown dog, and she found this amusing. Sherry Lee asked whether or not I owned a dog or ever had one, and while I answered yes, we did have a dog many years ago, I told her in no way did our dog resemble the one she was drawing. Our only dog, Benson, was a large black and white bearded collie, and I have wonderful visions of Noel and Ben romping together on the other side, much the way they did in our backyard in Pennsylvania. However, as Sherry Lee continued to draw, I began to laugh myself, because what she was drawing was a pretty good likeness of Stephanie's new dog, Ella, a chocolate Lab who tended to stay close to me when I was around her. Sherry Lee added that brown is also the color associated with setting up a home or building a nest. She asked if I were involved in anything like that, and I told her that I was busy establishing a second home in North Carolina. Finally, she indicated that I was working on a creative project. She said, "I can see that at this time you are simply gathering information, researching. However, the real creative touches will be made in August of 2005 as the project comes to a close." I told her that I was in the process of writing a book, and she simply smiled and nodded. Obviously the time frame she saw for the completion of the book was way off...perhaps mediums tend to ignore procrastination.

When I met MD at the end of the day, she asked how I felt about these readings, and my first response was, "They weren't as dramatic as before." She turned, looked at me, and said, "Maybe you don't need them as badly as before." The comment was an echo of Martie's thoughts, and upon reflection, I believe both women were right. The first time I went to Lily Dale, my grief was without boundaries, all-consuming, and I know that just as those who sat on the porch the first night felt the intensity of my sadness, so did Noel, choosing immediately to let me know he was all right. The second time I engaged the spiritual world through Martie, the reading was very meaningful, touching upon my foray into the past by way of old photos. Noel again gave me messages to support my hope that he was still around and observing what I was doing with my life. This time, however, the message was more subtle. It didn't focus upon me because my needs *had* diminished, and in many respects my dependency on Lily Dale had dwindled as well. After all, how many times can one climb the same mountain, feeling the wild exhilaration she first felt upon reaching the top?

I am sure I will return sometime in the future to the small village that gave me so much insight, much as anyone might hope to return to where she experienced the profound and extraordinary. For now, I am content to draw my strength from within, as well as from my family and friends as we all move forward, knowing without qualification that we are being tended to by Noel. As Martie said, "This is a good thing."

TWENTY-EIGHT

john edward: out of bed and up close

He who can no longer pause to wonder and
stand rapt in awe is as good as dead;
his eyes are closed.
-Albert Einstein

In an earlier chapter I indicated the impact John Edward and his program, *Crossing Over*, had upon me when sorrow had struck like an unexpected tsunami. As I look back I can now acknowledge how overwhelming those first months were despite, or perhaps because of, the messages I believed were coming from Noel. There were so many times when I thought I must be losing my mind. My nocturnal trysts with John Edward every night at eleven o'clock helped push back those feelings of fear, because for one hour I could transport myself, through the medium of television, onto the set with others who were in as much pain as I was. It must certainly be true that misery does love company, and maybe my obsessive devotion to losing myself every night at eleven indicated my diminished capacity for what was real at the time. Make no mistake, however; this man and all that he represents provided what I desperately needed then. I was receiving messages from my husband, and, crazy or not, I wasn't about to disregard them because when I turned on that television, I could see my situation mirrored several times over. Real craziness back then would have been to ignore what was before me.

In the spring of 2006, I went onto the Internet to check on the cross-country tour that John Edward was making, and I discovered to my delight that he was going to be in Charleston, South Carolina in a few weeks. By then I was very much ready to see this man in person, cost of the ticket be damned! Once again my sidekick and stalwart friend Marge was the one to accompany me on this pilgrimage. She had no desire to see the program but was quite willing to go with me to Charleston and make it a girls' overnight gala. Finally, I was going to be 'on the set' rather than viewing *Crossing Over* from my bedroom. I was euphoric!

We left Beaufort right after lunch for a trip that takes an hour and forty-five minutes to complete. As I drove I had the opportunity to think about what I expected to gain from this adventure. In my mind I spoke to Noel and told him that, realistically, I knew the chances of John's coming to me with a reading were very slim. After all, I had enjoyed the benefits of being with two different mediums in one-on-one situations, and to expect further validation from the likes of John Edward was pushing my luck. However, I did mention to my husband that if it were at all possible, I wouldn't mind some kind of sign from him to let me know he was observing. A pretty tall order, I suppose, but by now you must realize I often posed that request to Noel, hoping for the best.

When I was six, my Dad who was a very skilled electrician, built a television from a kit. I can remember that, despite being pretty much mesmerized by what I saw on that very small screen, none of it felt real. Today television still remains something of an enigma in that reality is, more often than not, stretched beyond the normal boundaries. Consider, then, that I was seeing someone on the screen who claimed to be able to speak to the spirits of those who have crossed over to the next life. This is what I had to weigh in my anxious mind as I watched *Crossing Over* every night. Now I was about to see the real person, no off and on switch, no commercials.

Marge and I arrived in Charleston, checked into our hotel, and then did some shopping. After we had dinner, I proceeded to the hotel where John was appearing, and, naturally, a line had formed at the entrance to the ballroom where the program was being held. I spoke with the people in front of me as well as those behind. We exchanged stories, and while that part of the evening is somewhat vague now, I do remember thinking we all were very much alike in our belief in life on the other side. All of us had had some kind of experience that validated our beliefs, and my hearing those stories was reinforcement I continued to seek.

When we finally got in and were seated, I was surprised the room wasn't larger. My guess is that it held around two hundred people, and every seat was occupied. I managed to secure a seat in the center section, just three rows away from the stage, and when the host came from behind the curtains, I couldn't quite believe I was actually that close to him.

Having observed John on a television screen for all those months, I was pleased to see he was every bit as charismatic as I had believed him to be years ago when everything was in turmoil. His mode of dress was totally informal, jeans and a shirt that he didn't tuck in, and his interaction with the audience was equally informal. John was friendly, personable, and witty, and I found I was as entranced as I had been all those nights when his show offered much-needed relief.

I can say, without reservation, every reading I observed that evening was believable. Furthermore, the reactions of those whom John singled out to receive messages were spontaneous and real. A woman sitting beside me was given a reading, and as I listened to her speaking with her friend afterward, there was no doubt in my mind the exchange had been authentic. She talked about specific places and people she believed John was referencing, in particular an aunt who had passed over. Across the room, an attractive young woman was given an especially poignant reading. John indicated that someone close to her had recently been killed, and that a famous individual had been involved in the accident. It turned out her fiancé had been part of the sound crew that had accompanied a well-known band on a road trip a few months before, and he was killed in a small plane crash.

Did I receive a reading? Well, not exactly. However, true to my husband's customary way of communicating, the message I got was a bit more subtle. What I am about to recount involved some deliberation on my part because it is very personal. However, nothing is to be gained at this point by tantalizing the reader, only to come up short. From the time Noel and I were married, he, with his droll sense of humor, decided to name my body parts, and while I won't divulge every detail of this little game, I will simply say that two were named Betty and Barbara.

John was providing a reading to a woman a couple of rows behind where I was sitting, and I was hanging on to every word. He paused at one point, then started to laugh and asked her whether or not a particular word held any significance for her. Her face turned red, and she started to stammer. John broke into a full-blown laugh, told her not to be embarrassed, because most people indulged in giving pet names for body parts, then proceeded to say that his family had names for the genitals of both male and female. "In my family," he said, "the male genitalia was called Walter and the female named Betty." Everyone began to laugh, and perhaps I laughed the longest. Coincidence? Maybe, but remember John Edward doesn't believe in coincidence, so for brief moment I let that little bit of humor be meant for me, my nugget to take home.

Just like seeing Josh Groban in concert, being with John Edward in person was another part of a picture I continue to create, a work of art that has evolved slowly and has become a mural, a panorama of sorts. This mural stretches around the walls of my mind, and it provides a place where I can retreat and contemplate my life without the man who made my former existence so rich. Both Groban and Edward provided a connection early on that helped pull me out of despair and place me on a path of healthy acceptance. The experiences I associate with both men added richness and texture to my new life.

In April of 2001, I would never have exchanged my life with Noel for the one I have now. Almost two decades later, however, I recognize I was given opportunities that provided me with strength to transport myself, albeit slowly, out of a place of darkness and into one of light. Those opportunities became revelations that were the brick and mortar with which I built the foundation of my new life.

TWENTY-NINE

rewriting the script

The most painful state of being is remembering the future,
particularly the one you will never have.
-Anonymous

We have all heard people acquiesce to an untenable situation with the words, "I guess you just have to play with the hand you are dealt." While somewhat trite, the assumption is often accurate. The time will never come that I totally banish from my mind my husband's passing. After nearly two decades I still think about Noel, and I am reminded of the loss I sustained. But when the days continue to march by, and you are carried farther away from the epicenter of shock, you still have to play the hand you are dealt. It is how you play it that matters…mostly for you.

There was a time a few years ago when I sat listening to a deeply philosophical presentation, and the speaker addressed the hypothesis that "we are here to work on our souls." The concept resonated with me, and the thought went through my mind, "Is this simply another way to state that we are learning to play with the hands we are dealt?" Afterward, I talked with the presenter, and I suggested that as self-absorbed as it might seem, I wondered whether or not the loss of my husband is intended to be part of my soul's work. Again, I defer to Mitch Albom whose novel, *The Five People You Meet in Heaven,* has become a Bible of sorts for me. Albom writes, "Sacrifice is a part of life. It's supposed to be. It's not something to regret. Sometimes when you sacrifice something precious, you're not really losing it. You're just passing it on to someone else."

Occasionally I let myself wonder about what my life might have been like if Noel were with me today. These daydreams vary and have long since lost their painful dimension, often focusing, instead, on sentimental moments. However, sentimentality becomes a little testy when I am forced to undertake those jobs that normally were done by Noel This includes the time when I stood on a ladder in my bedroom, trying to install a blind, cursing my inability to hold the blind in one hand and the screwdriver in the other, wondering how I was supposed to insert the screw. My fix-it skills are sadly wanting, and I discovered that no amount of swearing provided a third hand to help put up that blind. And just recently, when a limb six inches in diameter came through the roof of my house, imbedding itself with the vengeance of a thrown javelin, I found myself looking up and wondering why my late husband couldn't have exerted just a little effort to sweep that limb to the side.

Would I have preferred to have Noel by my side for many more years? Of course I would, but with the understanding that he could enjoy good health and the ability to live life to the fullest. Scenes from the film *On Golden Pond* used to drift through my mind occasionally, and the knowledge that I would never experience my husband as an older man was painful. Stephanie and I used to spend countless hours discussing the profound changes that came about in both of us after we lost her father. She insists, however, that we came to accept our loss with grace and without rancor, and that both of us are able to see more positive than negative in our lives. I tend to agree…most of the time.

I had an occasion to communicate with a journalist in San Francisco regarding an article he had written, and I was pleasantly surprised when he responded to my letter, saying, "May your path be continuously refreshing and bewildering and true." I would like to tell him now that perhaps this wish was prophetic, because all of those words describe where I am in my journey today. Noel's passing put me in a place I never would have sought. It was brutal and debilitating; however, it did not defeat me. Most important, my journey on this road is very much bound to the truths that will let me see Noel once more, and that makes all the difference in how I am trying to live out the remainder of my life. This includes, of course, a little help from my guy over there.

It has been over nineteen years since my life was turned upside down. For those of us who suffer the loss of a person we love without reservation, the passage of time blunts the pain, and we accept that divesting ourselves of grief entirely is an elusive quest. Certainly there is no easy solution. As confounded as we may be by that reality, coping with the here and now is essential for healthy living and must become our new approach. I like to believe somewhere in the ethereal realm where Noel now resides, disease and pain are nonexistent, and that belief provides me with comfort. Along the way I discovered when I cried-and make no mistake, I cried for many years-it was not always for Noel, because I came to believe he is fine. I cried, instead, for myself and for my loneliness. What helped me as I continued slogging through my own emotional swamp, was the recognition that my husband was no longer suffering the ravages of his leukemia. It takes a while to reach the 'it's-not-all-about-me' stage, but that's all right. I know now the most important gifts I gave to my husband included my attempts to help him fight for his life here and the manner in which I helped him cross to his new life in a better place. However, there is a third gift that I must continue to offer: the honor I accord Noel's memory by carrying on with my own life in a way that would make him proud of me. A large part of dealing with my grief was predicated upon the occasional signs that I received, signs that some will always contend are simply wishful thinking on my part. I refused to accept that contention then, nor do I accept it now. Maybe it was stubborn determination that helped me cope when life seemed hopeless.

One fascinating aspect of having written this book is the fact that just when I think I have arrived at the conclusion and am composing the final lines, something else comes to mind that I think might provide substance as well as comfort for the reader. It is almost as though my story has taken on a life of its own and doesn't want to conclude. What follows are a couple more subtle nudges that made me happy at the time and still delight me when I think about them.

The year was 2009. The very dear couple I alluded to earlier and traveled with extensively after Noel passed away, suggested a month-long cruise through the South Pacific, and I jumped at the opportunity. I need to take a moment here to discuss my relationship with Walt and Nancy. These are two people whose kindness and friendship I cannot stress enough. They simply are the best friends a person could hope for. So often they invited me to be with them when they traveled, whether on a short trip, or on the many cruises I enjoyed because they included me; which brings me to the incident when we docked at Maui.

It was mid-morning and the ship was edging into the harbor. The three of us had gone out onto one of the upper decks to watch. As we approached, I could see a long expanse of large rubber tires attached to the side of the berth. From a distance the look was that of a solid black wall of rubber 'Os', with the exception of one tire. That tire had fairly large white letters printed on it, and as we pulled closer, I looked down on those letters which were four in number…NOEL! The three of us looked at one another, and we simply shook our heads. I asked myself at the time why we chose that side of the ship as our point of observation; we could just as easily been on the opposite side and missed that single bit of writing completely.

On a later cruise through the North Atlantic, the three of us were leaving the Crow's Nest after having had some wine, and we were headed for dinner. Walt and I were walking ahead, and we noticed Nancy was lagging behind. I turned around and said, "Come on slow poke," but then noticed she was in tears. I went back to her right away, and after getting her breath, she said, "I saw Noel walking beside you two. It was as clear as day." Both of these people have had similar experiences that did not involve me; they are no strangers to such incidents.

As surely as the heat wanes marginally in the South and the leaves become brilliant in the North, autumn brings about football season, a game played in every state, both college and professional; for some of us it is all-consuming. Noel and I lived thirty-five years in Pittsburgh, and for most of that time we were diehard Steeler fans. You simply cannot live in or near that city and be anything else. I became a football junkie out of necessity, knowing if I wanted to spend Sunday afternoons in the fall with my husband, I had to join the ranks of fans, and in many respects I became a more devoted one than he. When we arrived in South Carolina we found a group of transplanted Pittsburghers, real Steeler fans, and our autumn Sundays were filled with the bliss only those who are decked in black and gold can fully understand. We purchased a black golf cart, and the first accoutrements for this wonderful machine were a Steeler flag and a large Steeler logo for the front. This is the backdrop for an additional tweak from the other side.

I was in Greenville, South Carolina with Jennifer and her family, and we were watching another Pittsburgh season unfold. It was a close game, and we were all yelling and cheering for our team, just as we had always done. I went into the kitchen to get something to drink, and as I stood there, momentarily alone, I couldn't help but tell Noel how good it would be if he were with us, cheering the loudest, even using language sometimes less than appropriate for small ears. I briefly acknowledged once more how much I yearned to know for certain he knew we were doing well and still enjoying what we had always enjoyed as a family. I should have known by then he was with us. Returning to the game, I sat down, and Sydney came to me immediately.

Holding a crayon in one hand and a piece of paper in the other, she said, "Nana, I am drawing this football for Pop Pop." Sweet little Sydney still retained that diaphanous thread of connection. No one had mentioned Noel's name during the day, and yet she thought of him. Her spontaneous gesture was sufficient to make me believe Noel had heard my wish and gave me a quick nod.

Not long after I stood at my kitchen window, watching leaves from the live oak trees make their twirling descent to the ground. These majestic giants that sprawl across the Lowcountry of South Carolina reinforce my belief in the powerful force that holds sway over our universe. My first thought that day, however, was much less ethereal as I bemoaned the fact that even though I had just paid my neighbor's son to remove the leaves from my property, I could barely see my lawn. In the North we had three to four weeks of heavy leaf raking in the fall before winter set in. Here the oak trees seem to be in a state of perpetual shedding, and any hope of getting ahead of the raking is usually futile. My next thought, however, was considerably more philosophical. My stereo was playing in the background, and of course, it was Josh Groban, my musical companion and spiritual transporter, who provided the backdrop for my musings that morning. As I gazed out the window, it occurred to me that those leaves, brown and leathery, had their own beauty and grace. They fluttered about randomly, and I thought to myself each leaf is much like the human body that must be discarded as the soul is carried forth on the wind. New leaves appear quietly, almost immediately and without fanfare, as the old ones become a part of the earth. The age-old process continues. By the way, these moments of musing did not bring with them any indication Noel had heard or that he agreed.

I know eventually I will close the pages of this book; yet I am certain there will be ongoing chapters of my life that will include my late husband. Revelations and incidents will happen, and I will commit them to paper, a postscript for myself. I quietly acknowledge there is no real conclusion to the story, because I am determined to keep open those channels of communication that have served me well and brought me into a special place called hope.

I would never suggest living life as a widow is simple-nothing could be more erroneous. The complexities we are handed, along with our husband's death certificate, are numerous and difficult. I am saying, however, that every widow who wants to move through her pain to a tranquil spot where she might gain the courage to move forward, has the capacity to do so. A young sixteen year old girl, Karita Jackson, wrote this on an Outward Bound Flier: "Mentally I've discovered that what lies ahead of me or what lies behind me is nothing compared to what lies within me now." So I ask of all widows, look within yourself to find your strength that is most certainly there. Know this without a doubt: with enough determination, you will discover this treasure, and it is yours for the taking. God speed your efforts!

THIRTY

setting myself free

There came a time when the risk to remain tight in the bud was more painful than the risk it took to blossom.
-Anais Nin

It was my younger daughter who often voiced her concern, saying I needed to move forward with my life, and by that she meant I should seek a male companion. I guess when the idea of a dog didn't take root, she got right to the heart of the issue. Furthermore, at one point she had in mind just the person, but suggested that *we* needed to go about this slowly and judiciously because the man in question had just become a new widower, and his pain was still very evident. While it may seem strange that the child who was so close to her father would even think of trying to match me up with a man, truth be known, my children may know me better than I know myself.

As I indicated in an earlier chapter, in quiet moments of clarity I admitted I did yearn for male companionship. I could not see myself in another marriage, and there was a time when I couldn't imagine intimacy with another man. Nevertheless, as I continued to move father away from my loss, there was part of me that wistfully wanted to have someone with whom I could go to dinner and see a movie, a man who would discuss that movie, someone whose deep voice would be a welcome contrast to the females with whom I usually talked.

Shortly after Stephanie's attempt to generate a love life for me, I made plans to travel to North Carolina where I owned a home with my friend, Beverly. Back then, when I drove any length of time alone, I tended to talk to Noel in my mind and aloud as well. This time of sharing thoughts, despite the fact that he was not physically with me, didn't surprise or concern me, because when he and I traveled together, we invariably had an ongoing conversation until we arrived at our destination. We never seemed to run out of things to talk about, and both of us recognized that over the years, within the confines of our automobile, we solved a lot of problems requiring extended time for in-depth discussion.

It was on this three hour drive that I spoke to Noel about the empty place in my life only a male could fill. I told him it couldn't be just any man, and quite frankly, no man could assume the role he had played in my life. Then I added, "Noel, I need to know this is something you understand, something you want for me as well." I hadn't traveled two miles farther when I observed a road sign trumpeting the last name of the gentleman my daughter seemed to feel was destined to meet me and sweep me off my feet! For the sake of discussion, I am going to use the name Asher, although that is not his real name. So there it was to my right, Asher Lane. I started to laugh and said to Noel, "You have to be kidding!" A quarter of a mile farther on, there it was once more, Asher Lane. Apparently the road made a loop and merged back onto the highway. By then I was paying a little more attention, and the second sign sent me into a fit of giggles.

By itself, this incident could be seen as simple irony, and even I would have called it a coincidence. However, my husband was never one for small talk or unimportant detail. The following day I was on the road again after having spent the night with my friend. She and I were driving separate cars to North Carolina, and since we were on a road totally unfamiliar to me, she was leading the way. At one point I noticed a huge, bright yellow real estate sign, sitting off in a field. The agency's name was written in bold letters that must have been three feet tall, Asher Real Estate. The sign stood by itself; there were no competitors on that landscape, no other advertisement. I laughed to myself, a little nervously I might add, and I said to Noel, "All right, my dear, this is getting just a little weird." The entire trip took me through countryside I had never traveled before, and by this time I was beginning to think perhaps I had entered a different time warp, maybe the Twilight Zone. It seemed obvious to me I was being given some kind of a message. Imagine then how I felt when ten miles later there was another road sign, this time indicating I was on Asher Road! Really? Imagine that! When Beverly and I finally reached our house in Hendersonville, North Carolina and were sitting over a glass of wine, I told her about my experiences, both the day before and during our trip that day.

The following day we met with Jane, a mutual friend, for lunch in Asheville, and she said she would like to show us the place where she had set up a small booth for antiques. She turned to Beverly and said, "I don't know if you remember the location, but it is in the Asher Building." Beverly looked at me and said, "Do you still have doubts?"

I look back on this incident from the vantage point of being well into my second decade without Noel. Mr. Asher never became a part of my life; in fact I never met the man. However, life still presents those times when I pause to take stock of where I am presently and where I might be going. I don't let myself become bogged down by my recollections after eighteen years, particularly now that I have someone in my life who helps me to ward off any lingering sadness I might experience. I will point out to you, however, that anyone who says time heals all wounds fails to mention that the scars, however faint, still remain, and they do occasionally ache.

I joined a group of women writers a few years after Noel passed away; at that point I had begun writing my memoir. I stayed with the group on a regular basis for several years, and they were instrumental in coaching and encouraging me as I continued to bring forth my story. Furthermore, they gave me the impetus to return to my book with some of the enthusiasm I lost along the way. During one gathering, I told them about the signs I felt Noel had given to me regarding male companionship. At the conclusion of the meeting, one of the members and a very dear friend-my other Stephanie-sought me out and said, "Up until this time, I thought you would never seek another man. I guess I believed that you felt so strongly about having the one love of your life, and that was it." She then went on to say something that I hadn't thought about: "I think it is time for you to finish your book and put it to rest," she continued. "You have reached another phase in your life, and finishing the book will simply get more difficult if you let it drag on."

I thought about her comments after I returned home, and I believe she offered sound advice. Closure on the life I had spent with Noel until the time of his passing will never be entirely attainable, nor have I ever sought that. On the other hand, bringing my book to its conclusion is something I can achieve, and it is necessary that I make every effort to do so. Failure to complete what I consider a message of the optimism for others who are facing what I encountered after the loss of my husband is unacceptable; furthermore, paying tribute to the most important man in my life for four decades is very important to me. In the years I spent writing about my loss, the book became a compilation of the love I always felt for Noel, and that did not cease with his passing. If anything, the very text I produced made it more poignant! I channeled my feelings into the next best thing, a truthful account of my love *and my grief*, and a testimonial to the man whose life and death made me the person I am today. The book became my lover, the object of my passions and sentiments. I have chosen to go on with a life that is rewarding in so many ways; thus I must finish my writing and continue to move beyond the final words of the book. This move will not always be easy because my heart will retain some aspect of the heaviness that only the loss of one so deeply loved can produce.

I have alluded in passing to the man who has been with me for almost ten years. I made it very clear from the time we began our life together I would never look at him as a replacement for my late husband. That would be delusional of me and terribly unfair to him. I am a very different person than I was when Noel passed away, and this man is his own person. I make no comparisons, and I accept with gratitude the warmth and comfort he has provided in his own way. That I can love again is a gift, and I urge every widow to consider embracing love once more. Your life has potential to be much richer.

Perhaps it is part of my life-plan that when I was blindsided by loss, my growth had to include working through my sadness and coming out on the other side a much stronger person. Being free to love and be loved is a very precious gift. It was Michaelangelo who said, "I saw the angel in the marble, and I carved until I set him free."

POST SCRIPT

heartfelt thanks

The human body experiences a powerful gravitational pull in the direction of hope. That is why the patient's hopes are the physician's secret weapon. They are the hidden ingredient in any prescription.

-anonymous

If I failed to address the medical people who were there for Noel and me, before his passing as well as after, it would be an inexcusable oversight. When we started down the long road that eventually diverted my husband's path away from mine, there were several people whose sensitivity and genuine affection for both of us went well beyond the relationship of medical caretaker and patient. To have found these individuals during a time of such intense physical and emotional distress is nothing short of miraculous, and they will always occupy a special place in my heart.

The list is lengthy. There were the nurses at Johns Hopkins who were with us the first time Noel was hospitalized there.

When they saw he had returned and was located in another unit, they came to visit him. There are not sufficient words of praise for the nurses who cared for him during the thirteen days he lay comatose. They talked to him, washed his hair, massaged his legs, and treated him with more tenderness and sensitivity than I could have imagined. I saw them quite literally as his guardian angels here on earth.

There was a counselor, Nyla, who miraculously appeared by my side within fifteen minutes of Noel's terrifying collapse into his private darkness. Not only did she stay with me that first day, but she also remained with me throughout the thirteen torturous days when my life had spun out of control. I will always think of her devotion to my well-being as a gift of love from one human to another rather than the routine sympathy of a young woman simply doing her job.

And, of course, there were those with whom I forged a lifelong bond, people who let me cling to them like the terrified innocent I was, staying with me when there was hope as well as during the darkest hours when that hope was dashed. These young shamans bolstered me after Noel's passing when I could have been just one more statistic, a woman whose misfortune was losing her husband, something they see all the time. Reflection two decades later continues to underscore my belief these people are somehow part of a greater plan, holding our lives in their hands when necessary. What I had to accept then, however, was that the gods are sometimes powerless and there are no guarantees, even when you are dealing with the best of the best.

Let me begin with Dr. Douglas Thompson. Every person who is ill, as well as those who are healthy, should have as his or her internist a Doug Thompson. At the time he came into our lives, he was a very young physician, but then I have come to accept that Noel's fate, and by default, mine, was placed in the hands of many fresh and brilliant young minds whose focused dedication to the patient had not become jaded.

Dr. Thompson is the physician who diagnosed Noel in 1999 as the result of a routine examination and the accompanying blood tests. It was the first time they had met, and we discovered over the next few days Doug was very much impacted by the news he had to deliver to my husband. The day Noel came home with the verdict that would forever change our lives, Doug called late in the afternoon to see how both of us were doing. His first words to me were, "I can't believe that I met Noel for the first time today and had to give him this kind of news!" I could hear the genuine dismay in his voice, and as terrible as I felt, my heart went out to him. That he kept close tabs on us during the ensuing months is an understatement. There was a time I went to him because I felt that depression was becoming a part of my daily existence, no matter how hard I tried to ward it off. I remember I broke down in his office and sobbed, saying I didn't think I could go through losing Noel. He was at my side immediately and put his arm around me, saying that we would all work our way through this. He could have been my son, and indeed I came to think of him as the son I would never have. He provided the reassurance I so desperately needed then, and I will never forget the compassion he extended then and so many times after.

In 2001, a few weeks after Noel passed away, Doug called and said he was running a race for Team in Training, a group that sponsors events for the Leukemia and Lymphoma

Society. The race was to be held in Nashville, Tennessee, and Doug planned to run in memory of Noel. This became a pivotal moment in my recovery because it gave me something concrete to which I could devote my time and energies on Noel's behalf. I had worked so hard during the months he was ill, and yet I had failed to accomplish what I wanted most, the restoration of my husband's health. Here was another chance to prove myself, not only for Noel, but also for the cause of eradicating leukemia. What a wonderful gift young Doug Thompson gave to me! I threw myself into raising money to support his race, and between the two of us, we brought in over eight thousand dollars.

The most heartfelt part of that effort came, however, when I went to Nashville to watch Dr. Doug run. It was his first race of this length, twenty-six plus miles, and despite the amount of time he had invested in readying himself, I knew it would be a challenge. At one point I stood at the twenty-one mile marker and waited for him to come through. After half an hour I thought perhaps I had missed him and was about to leave when I glanced back through the throng of runners and saw him. My heart sank because he looked so beaten; he later told me he had really run into a wall at that point and didn't know if he could make it to the finish line. I started to yell, to encourage him, and I received a weak smile in return as he ran by. It struck me then that I had to have a picture of this young man's devotion to the commitment he had made, so I started to run after him, unaware I had placed myself in the midst of the athletes. At that point it didn't make any difference; I simply knew I had to get far enough ahead of Doug to record forever the effort he was expending to keep Noel's memory alive. So there I was, running as if my life depended upon it, passing other runners. In the background I could hear people cheering and laughing. I am sure that sight wasn't anything one will ever encounter in a runner's journal, but run I did. I finally got far enough ahead of him to stop, take my one snap-shot, and pray I didn't drop over from a heart attack right there. Later, when I sent out thank you notes to all who had contributed to this effort, I included that picture of Doug. Fortunately there was no record of the photographer who must have looked to some like a deranged lunatic as she rushed headlong through those runners.

I returned to the finish line, along with Doug's family, to await his final push across. I discovered the last five miles of a race of this length is a long wait. However, he did finish, and when he came around the final turn, my tears were non-stop. I cried tears of gratitude that someone would invest so much of himself for Noel, and I cried tears of sadness that it had to be this way. I had asked Noel at the beginning of the race to give this young warrior wings, and I am certain he did. Many times after I watched Doug compete in other rac-es, and always my heart went with him, knowing Noel must be so happy to have such wonderful representation. Years later Doug Thompson continues to run for leukemia; he has been in races across the desert in Chile and the snow-packed terrain near the North Pole. My guess is that the heavens continue to cheer him on. On a final note, he left his prac-tice in Beaufort and went on to become an oncologist. He told me his incentive was, in part, his experience with Noel and me. It doesn't get any better than that.

When Noel was first diagnosed, I decided we would not fight a disease this serious in the small town where we had retired. After a brief period of emotional paralysis, I emerged ready to take on Chronic Lymphocytic Leukemia. I knew thirty plus years of my professional life had been spent in an environment where research was common; thus I was going to find a way to navigate us through this dark valley. Noel downplayed the seriousness of the disease, but this was usually his approach to life's challenges. Contrary to the contention that men can be such babies when they are ill, Noel chose to slog his way through any health issue with silent determination.

My investigation of the best medical facilities in the country was greatly enhanced by communication with my husband's cousin, a cancer research doctor who had worked for Sloan-Kettering. His information provided a great deal of hope as I started down the unfamiliar road of blood cancer. Finally we settled on Johns Hopkins Cancer Research Center and Dr. Ian Flinn, a CLL specialist. It was the best decision I could have made during this stressful period. Like Doug Thompson, Ian was a young man, and even younger looking, so much so that I referred to him as the "Doogie Howser" of cancer treatment. Although he was unable to save Noel, and I am convinced now that no one could have done so, I am pretty certain finding Dr. Flinn was a preordained part of the greater picture I often reference. Ian and his physician's assistant, Jennifer, became not only potential life savers but also good friends, people who made me understand I could call any time I had questions or concerns. Noel and I were never just numbers. The way these people maintained an ongoing relationship with those they treated is testament to their dedication.

When we first met with Dr. Flinn there was, at the time, great potential for gene therapy as a combatant for CLL, and we placed all of our hopes in this basket. I created a paper-weight for him with the picture of a celebrity dressed in very revealing cut-off jeans shorts and included the words, 'Stick with jean therapy'. I was told later this made his day, and he laughed aloud when receiving it. However, the trials that were supposed to be forthcoming were put on hold instead, while Noel's health continued to deteriorate. In spite of this, Ian always gave us reason to be confident. When Noel was admitted to the hospital for what would be the final time, Ian took me into a room to tell me that the disease had taken a radical turn for the worse, but even then, he didn't just drop this news and leave me alone. The number of times he came to my husband's room, as he lay heavily sedated, to talk not only to me but also to Noel, was reinforcement that gave me the will to continue believing my husband still had every chance of recovery. Of course, many will assert this is, after all, what all doctors should do. However, after Noel passed away, Dr. Flinn continued to stay in touch, and he made it clear I should contact him whenever I needed to do so.

During the December following Noel's passing I had an opportunity to attend a conference where Ian was making a presentation. I entered at the rear of the auditorium where he was speaking and took a seat. After he was finished, I made my way to the front where many people had gathered around, waiting on the fringes as one person after another sought him out, hoping to have a brief word with him. However, when he spied me, he stopped speaking and moved through the crowd to where I stood. When he smiled and opened his arms for a hug, I was consumed with emotion. This was the young man who had seen me through the most horrific time of my life, and I wasn't just another statistic to him. It is no overstatement to say Ian Flinn was decidedly an important part of my being able to move forward at a time when it would have been easy to give up.

The first time Noel and I went to Johns Hopkins was in January of 2000. It was a cold bitter day in Baltimore, and despite the fact that Noel was feeling well and looked very healthy, the chill extended to my inner core, the place where fear is born. We both laughed nervously about the location of Dr. Flinn's office, down in the bowels of a building where we had to walk through long passages that were walled on either side in stone. Noel joked about the place appearing to be a medieval tomb and asked if I thought we would ever get out. Later we were told a new facility was to open within the next year, a beautiful building that would have all the latest technology and be pleasing to the eye. I would come to know the new building very well before our time in Baltimore came to a close.

After completing all the necessary paperwork, we met a girl, young enough to be our daughter who, in fact, shared our older daughter's name. Jennifer Sickler was very upbeat as she explained gene therapy and how the trials were to be conducted, and it was she who described to Noel what he would have to do in order to participate when the trials were started. Finally she said, "You will have to provide several vials of blood today." My husband, the man who came close to fainting the first time he attempted to give blood at a school-sponsored drive replied, "Bring on the vampires!" From that point on Jen and Noel were fast friends. Later I came to think of her as another daughter who was there for me so often when I needed reassurance. Her immediate response to the questions I fired at her in e-mails became a lifeline for me.

The first time Noel was hospitalized at Hopkins was in February of 2001, six weeks before he passed away. Jennifer made it a point to come up from her lab and see him at least every other day. This meant a great deal to him and to me as well. One time, after she had left the room, I commented on how good she was to take time out and visit. Noel's response was, "Yes, and she has a great bod, too!" I laughed and said she almost qualified as jail bait, so he had better settle down. After he passed away, I had occasion to be with Jennifer, and I told her about my husband's observation. Rather than being put off, she laughed, saying she knew there were a lot of reasons she loved that man. This was simply one more human touch this medical team so naturally and lovingly bestowed, and it made all the difference in the world when the excruciating blow of finality was dealt.

All of these young people did what they do best in an attempt to save my husband from the disease that took his life. Each in his and her own way made Noel believe every time he saw them that he was important, not just any patient but an individual who deserved their respect. If bedside manner and genuine empathy could be packaged and sold, these three could be billionaires. For whatever reason, Noel wasn't meant live through his ordeal; otherwise, I know that if a miracle were to have been part of the equation, the brilliance and dedication of these medical beacons would have brought it about. Very simply, they are the best medicine has to offer, and I will always be grateful for everything they did.

Every ending is just a beginning;
we just don't know it at the time.

-anonymous

ABOUT THE AUTHOR

 Retired high school English teacher, Carol Lucas, grew up in western Pennsylvania where she earned her bachelor's degree. She completed graduate work at the University of Notre Dame and the University of Pittsburgh. Carol began her career in 1964 in suburban Pittsburgh where she taught and lived for 35 years. During this time she also coordinated a high school Community Service Learning program. Upon retirement she received an Excellence in Teaching award from the state of Pennsylvania. Carol has since moved to Beaufort, South Carolina where she enjoys writing, golfing, and going on cruises- which she eagerly awaits resuming after the COVID pandemic rules are relaxed.

www.ingramcontent.com/pod-product-compliance
Lightning Source LLC
Chambersburg PA
CBHW051225060325
23075CB00005B/207